IS THE
BIBLICAL?

*Thinking through
the Toronto phenomenon*

Also by David Pawson:

Truth to Tell
The Normal Christian Birth
The Road to Hell
Fourth Wave
When Jesus Returns

IS THE BLESSING BIBLICAL?

Thinking through the Toronto phenomenon

J. David Pawson, MA, BSc

Foreword by
Nick Cuthbert

Hodder & Stoughton
LONDON SYDNEY AUCKLAND

British Library Cataloguing in Publication Data
A record for this book is available from the British Library.

ISBN 0 340 66147 X

Designed and typeset by Typograph, Irby, Wirral, Cheshire.
Printed and bound in Great Britain by Cox & Wyman Ltd,
Reading, Berkshire

Hodder and Stoughton Ltd
A division of Hodder Headline PLC
338 Euston Road
London NW1 3BH

Contents

Foreword

Tʜɪs is a book that had to be written and must be read! There is no doubt that something is going on. Some say it is a great move of the Spirit of God, others that it is a great deception, while many sense that elements of both may be present but are unsure how to articulate their concerns. This book will help.

There is a story in circulation about a ship at sea that picked up a signal of another vessel on its radar.

'We are on a collision course. Move over 20 degrees,' it signalled.

'Message received. You move over 20 degrees,' came the response.

Irritated by this, the ship responded, 'Obey my command. I am an Admiral. Move over!'

'I am an able seaman. Move 20 degrees to avoid collision,' came the reply.

'I am a battleship. Move immediately,' was the response.

'I am not moving,' came the reply. 'I am a lighthouse!'

God has given us a lighthouse in his Word and it stands there, unchanging, to keep us off the rocks and to guide us to safety. That is what this book is about. It isn't concerned with personalities or taking sides but it is about what it means to be biblical in faith and practice.

The way of the Bereans is still vital today, 'for they received the message with great eagerness and examined the Scriptures every day to see if what Paul said was true'. Paul told us to 'Test everything. Hold fast to the good' (1 Timothy 5:21). Again, he warned us, 'Keep watch over yourselves and the flock of which the Holy Spirit has made you overseers . . . savage wolves will come in among you and will not spare the flock' (Acts 20:28–30).

William Seymour, an elder at the Azuza Street Mission during the revival in the early part of this century, wrote, 'We are measuring every thing by the Word. Every experience must measure up to the Bible. Some say that is going too far, but if we have lived too close to the Word, we will settle that with the Lord when we meet him in the air.'

This insistence on Scripture being the yardstick by which we measure all that we are experiencing needs to be accompanied with courage to 'hold fast', as well as tempered with love so that we do not become harshly judgmental of one another. It is easy to become unloving while fighting for what we believe to be right. Nevertheless that should not prevent us from examining everything carefully. David Pawson writes in his usual forthright way and avoids these pitfalls. He does not hold back from challenging us to be wholly biblical but avoids being drawn into debate about specific places and people. We are left to draw our own conclusions.

We live in an age dominated by the idols of materialism (the love of things), hedonism (the love of pleasure), and narcissism (the love of self). The belief in absolutes has given way to everything being relative, and 'If it feels good, do it' has become the philosophy of the day. In this climate, which leaves countless people in such pain and emptiness, there is a quiet desperation to 'feel better'.

How easy for the idols and the philosophy of our time to permeate the Church even if disguised in religious clothes. There can be no other way to avoid this than to cling as closely as we can to God's revealed Word.

David takes us back to the Scriptures. Here we have a plumbline to find out if, in our hunger for more reality and experience, we have wandered from the true. It must be the Scriptures to which we should turn if we are to rediscover the Christianity of sacrifice, service and servanthood, and a faith that propels us out into a world that desperately needs to be touched with the truth and power of the Gospel. As David points out, it would be so sad if, at this time, our desire for experience pulls us away from the Scriptures, or our desire for biblical truth causes us to pull back from a full commitment to the work of the Holy Spirit. Here is a plea for a full biblical expression of Holy Spirit life in the Church today.

The erosion of the Bible as the test of the rightness of Christian practice may, in some circles, have been going on for some time. As one leader from outside the evangelical tradition commented recently, 'I am surprised at how lightly you evangelicals sit towards the Bible.'

David, in this book, is doing more than asking a few questions about certain unusual phenomena: he is sounding a warning note. Failure to heed it at this juncture could mean that in future, having wandered from our moorings, we are open to any wind of deception that will blow us where it wills.

David expresses a pastor's heart and rejoices in those who claim healing and release but writes out of concern for the many bewildered people in churches today who feel confused by much of what has been happening and are looking for leadership. A good shepherd seeks to protect his sheep from the wolves. If he wrote as an evangelist, he would rejoice in the testimonies of those who have become Christians but be concerned in case the present Church becomes an even greater irrelevancy than it already is in the eyes of many, by turning further in on itself rather than seeking to touch the lost.

But he writes primarily as a teacher, which he must do because that is his God-given gift to the Church. He not only brings us back to the book, but has an extraordinary ability to bring scholarly illumination in a simple way. His motive in writing is, I believe, the same as that of Paul when he wrote, 'I do not want you to be ignorant, brethren . . .' (1 Corinthians 12:1). Ignorance leads to manipulation and this book will help us to make sure we are well informed.

What David has written will cause us all to sit up and take stock. It will hopefully lead us to act with discernment, discipline and courage and not to confuse middle ground with compromise, nor questioning with opposition.

This book had to be written; now all that is left is to read it!

Nick Cuthbert

Speaking personally

'I've not been to Toronto.' I heard a rumour that this message is now appearing on T-shirts. If so, I qualify to wear one, since I have not been one of the thousands of pilgrims who have flocked to the Airport Vineyard Church in that city over the last eighteen months, either to observe or participate in the 'blessing'.

I haven't even been as far as the floor! Many will therefore question whether I am qualified to form an opinion, much less have the audacity to publish it.

There is a widespread notion that real knowledge has to be existential: something must be experienced before it can be examined or explained. If that is the case, I was wrong to write a book about heaven and hell, since I've never been to either. Perhaps this is one reason why so few preachers address these subjects.

Actually, the idea that something must be experienced before its merits or demerits can be assessed is as old as the Garden of Eden. Adam and Eve fell for it, though they already had God's Word, telling them all they needed to know.

We live in a society that is constantly seeking new

experiences, from trips on marijuana to trips to Majorca, from ouija boards to smorgasbords. This quest is fast extending into the spiritual realm with an increasing desire for sensual contact with the supernatural. This is hardly surprising, since God created human beings so that they 'would seek him and perhaps reach out for him and find him' (Acts 17:27).

But all spiritual experiences, however real they may be to those involved, are not necessarily the real thing. There are three primary sources: they may be genuinely from God, a fleshly substitute from man or a subtle counterfeit from Satan.

It has become customary to test experience in hindsight – that is, to see what the results are. 'By their fruit you will recognise them' (Matthew 7:20). But that verse is about discerning false prophets, not experiences. And the thrust of it is to look for their characteristic product *before* becoming involved with them. This book is based on the premise that the right approach for believers is to test all things before becoming involved with them, to look at the roots rather than the fruits.

The basic criterion must be what God has already said, as recorded in Scripture. In relation to any experience we need to ask the simple question: Has he clearly told us he wants us to have this by promising to give it to us? Once convinced that this is the case, we are at liberty, even under obligation, to seek it with all our heart.

By the mid-1960s I had become known as an 'evangelical'. As I understand that term, it refers to anyone for whom the Bible is the final authority on all matters of belief and behaviour. That was, and still is, one of my deepest convictions.

Then I became a 'charismatic', after an experience of being 'baptised in the Holy Spirit', which led to the exercise of some 'spiritual gifts'. This caused dismay among my 'evangelical' friends. I was said to have 'lost my critical faculties' and 'gone off the rails'. I was accused, with others, of 'building theology on experience' (though some critics clearly built theirs on their 'bad experience' of such things!).

I was the first speaker ever invited to address the National Assembly of the Evangelical Alliance on this issue – a case of a lion being thrown into a den of Daniels if ever there was one! My 'defence' then and subsequently was simple: that the experience was *biblical*.

I had actually come into it while preaching a lengthy series of sermons on 'The Holy Spirit, from Genesis to Revelation'. From this comprehensive study I became convinced that there was more to the biblical experience of the Spirit than I had yet enjoyed. Like John the baptiser, I came to see that Jesus has a twofold ministry, negative and positive: to take away the sin of the world and to baptise in the Holy Spirit (John 1:29,33). I sought and received.

I remained firmly evangelical. Many times since I have said publicly that I am not interested in any experience that is not rooted and grounded in Scripture. That is an essential principle both for my own pilgrimage and my ministry to others. If it's not in the Bible I can neither seek it nor teach it.

Now, thirty years later, I find myself batting at the other end, cautious rather than adventurous in relation to what others are experiencing, questioning what many see as a move, even 'the Move', of the Spirit in our generation. Some would see this as a hardening of my spiritual arteries, the conservatism of the elderly (yes, I am now an old-age pensioner!). I am no longer with-it. I've changed from radical to reactionary (my recent writings supporting the traditional understanding of hell and male leadership may confirm this).

I don't believe this to be the case. My hesitation springs from another source. In a recent book (*Fourth Wave*, Hodder and Stoughton, 1993), I shared my burden to see charismatics and evangelicals united in a balanced integration of Word and Spirit, as in the New Testament churches. In other words, theology (of the right kind) and experience (of the right kind) belong together and illuminate each other.

Until recently, there was an increasing rapprochement between them. But in what came to be labelled 'Third wave', I sensed the seeds of disintegration. Pragmatism crept in. If it works, it's right. The end justifies the means.

My impression of current events is that Word and Spirit are in real danger of drifting apart. My concern is not just that 'ministry' is understood as something that happens after preaching rather than during it or that teaching is being reduced, even omitted, in a number of meetings. It is the way Scripture is being made to fit what is happening rather than vice versa. Even worse is the dismissal of Scripture as irrelevant to the Spirit, who is 'free to act in non-biblical ways'. He is the Spirit of truth as well as power. He does not contradict himself. His inspired deeds of today will be consistent with his inspired words of yesterday. Neither his gifts nor his fruit have changed. We know the ways of the Spirit (as well as the works of the flesh and the devices of Satan) from the Scriptures he inspired (2 Timothy 3:16).

This is why I have not made any public statement about the 'blessing' until now, though many have pressed me to do so. I am basically what is known as a 'Bible teacher'. So far, I have not been able to find a clear biblical basis for what is being experienced and therefore felt unable to teach on it.

Yet now I feel compelled to break my silence. This has been precipitated by a number of factors, not least the use of my name in a press release and a circular letter to pastors without my knowledge or permission, both of which were almost totally negative in their attitude. This is not my position, as I trust readers will conclude.

It is unfortunate that much of the discussion has been polarised into 'for' and 'against'. This can only lead to division and a realignment of believers, particularly those in charismatic circles. I believe this is the result of asking the wrong question, namely: 'Is this movement of God or not?' This only allows the alternative answers of total approval or disapproval. This means in effect that those who have been 'blessed' are not disposed to question anything and those who haven't are not allowed to!

Rather, we should seek to discern what is of God and what isn't. It may well be that we should be talking about the 'Toronto mixed blessing'. For that we shall need more objective criteria than subjective testimony, though the latter must be taken into account.

Another reason I am writing is that it has become impossible to ignore the issue. The speed and scale with which the 'blessing' has spread, largely though not exclusively in charismatic and Pentecostal fellowships, confronts us with the need to make up our minds about it.

I want to help you to reach your own convictions rather than someone else's. One restraining influence on me thus far was the fear of being quoted as a kind of guru. I'd rather teach you *how* to think about things like this than *what* to think about them. Having been constantly asked by telephone and letter to make a pronouncement, I hope this book will not be treated as such.

It is not my last word on the subject. Rather is it intended to be a contribution to an ongoing debate. It is the first of my books to have a question as its title, which indicates my sense that there is more to say than I have said here. I believe my mind is still open to consider different answers to the question.

That does not mean that the thoughts expressed here are tentative. On the contrary, the direction of my thinking is quite clear, even if the destination is not. But the latter will only be reached through the former, even if later reflection promotes a change of course. That will only happen if I am provided with a more satisfactory interpretation of the scriptural data.

So I am writing *partly* for myself. It's time I 'came clean'. I did not want to be hasty in jumping to conclusions, especially since my personal exposure was limited, due to family and other circumstances. However, others have encouraged me to believe that what I am thinking and now saying needs to be heard, and heard as soon as possible. I bow to their judgment (and am grateful for the Foreword from one of them).

I am writing *particularly* for those who, like myself, have questions and reservations but often feel quite lonely, even hurt, because this is not an acceptable attitude in their group. Many have felt they must sever cherished relationships. I have talked to an ex-worship leader in a prominent Anglican church and an ex-associate pastor in a prominent Baptist church, both of whom felt they had to resign their positions. Others have stayed but felt the pain of being marginalised, spectators rather than participants in the fellowship.

I want to encourage them by articulating some of their difficulties, perhaps being a voice for a silent but sizeable minority. I want to reassure them that it's all right to ask questions, that we can trust our spirits and should not allow ourselves to be swept into anything about which we have doubts. I know from personal experience how much comfort comes from knowing that others have the same difficulties.

Most of the books already written have been very positive or very negative (chapter 8 in Rob Warner's *Prepare for Revival*, Hodder and Stoughton, 1995, came nearest to a critical assessment). I hope this volume will help to fill the gap between the two attitudes, which is where I believe many find themselves. But I am writing *primarily* for those already involved, either in receiving the 'blessing' or engaged in passing it on. This is an invitation to think, perhaps think again, about what is happening. It is as dangerous to leave the mind out of our experience as to leave the heart out of our theology. Holiness is holistic. Body, soul and spirit need to be integrated.

Let me say straight away that there is here no question about the reality of the experience which so many have had, though there is always the possibility of simulation (often the result of stimulation). What we are discussing here is the meaning and significance of that experience, which narrows the field of investigation.

I shall not be looking at the psychological aspects (others see the 'blessing' largely in terms of 'emotional release' and 'inner healing'). Nor will I be saying much about the pastoral implications (though the final chapter contains some guidance for the conduct of meetings). The historical aspects have been deliberately consigned to an appendix, whereas in other books this has been given a surprising prominence.

As the title suggests, the main focus is biblical. This is the fundamental issue both for me and for most of those who have sought my opinion. What does Scripture have to say, if anything, about the current phenomena?

Whether you finally agree or disagree with what you read, I dare to believe that it will do you nothing but good to reconsider your position in the light of the scriptural data which I believe relevant and which I have sought to interpret and apply.

I have attended three conferences on the subject, one

largely in favour and one largely against, while the third presented papers of different points of view. Thus I have tried to expose my thinking to a variety of attitudes. The disappointment has usually been in the failure to get to grips with the Bible itself. This, more than anything, prompted me to put my thoughts on paper.

May the Lord preserve us all from either missing or mistaking what he is doing among us.

David Pawson

CHAPTER 1

'Manifestations' and 'ministry'

IT HAS been suggested that I should begin with a brief description of what I'm talking about, although the 'Toronto blessing' (a nickname coined in England) is now so widespread and well known that few will need an explanation. And I would guess that those who buy this book will do so because they already know about it but are wondering what to think about it.

Much, though not all, of what broke out in the Airport Vineyard fellowship in Toronto early in 1994 was already happening in other locations, though not on the same scale. Toronto became a 'Mecca' for 'charismatic' pilgrims, especially exhausted pastors, seeking a renewed experience of the power and presence of God. They came from all over the world, but particularly from the British Isles, returning to spread the blessing (in four thousand churches so far, it is claimed).

That many have been blessed, few would question. The main effect has been to reinvigorate tired believers with a quickened interest in prayer, worship, Bible study and evangelism. There have been healings of the body, more frequently of damaged emotions. There have been some conversions and hope kindled for many people. Individuals have been transformed and churches brought to life. In other words, good things have happened.

So why should anyone have questions, much less reservations? To hesitate over getting involved is surely at best to miss what God is wanting or at worst to commit the unforgivable sin of ascribing the work of the Spirit to evil causes (Matthew 12:22–32). The fear of being guilty of either has led many to suppress their reservations, as has the genuine desire for every blessing available.

It must be emphatically stated that no true believer has problems with the concept of God blessing his people. On the contrary, that is exactly what he wants to do, has promised to do and may therefore be expected to do. He is a good God who only creates good things and wants to do good things for his creatures. Supremely in Christ he has *already* blessed believers with every spiritual blessing (Ephesians 1:3).

Jesus, the Son of this blessed and blessing God, also blessed people, especially those who were poor (he cursed the rich), those who were hungry (he cursed the well fed), those who weep (he cursed those who laugh) and those who were hated, ostracised and insulted because of their loyalty to himself (he cursed those who courted popularity and praise) – read Luke 6:20–26 for this startling version of the Beatitudes.

Both Old and New Testaments exhort God's people to bless others – and to bless him. The way to do this is the same as the way he blesses us, in actual words (Genesis 1:22,28). We bless God by praising him for his goodness to us (Psalm 103). We bless others by pronouncing his goodness on them, even if they are hostile to us (Matthew 5:44; Luke 6:28; Romans 12:14; 1 Corinthians 4:12).

So there can be nothing wrong with seeking blessing from God and others or seeking to give blessing to God and others, though we need to note that the primary means of this is verbal. There is power in words – both blessing and cursing. 'God bless you' is more than a wish, even more than a prayer. It could even be called a prediction. When uttered in faith, it becomes a channel of blessing.

So the idea of God blessing us, either directly or through others, is thoroughly biblical. And who can possibly object when there is more love for God and enthusiasm to do his will? So where is there a problem? Why should there be any doubts?

The answer lies in the *manner* in which the 'blessing' is currently being received and the *method* by which it is being communicated. These are highlighted in the widespread use of two words in a limited and specific way which does not appear to be consistent with their scriptural meaning. This raises the question as to whether they are being used to give a theological significance to behaviour which does not inherently warrant it.

Manifestations

The first word is 'manifestations', which is widely used to describe the physical actions accompanying reception of the 'blessing', ranging from the unusual to the extraordinary, the banal to the bizarre.

The most common is falling (from slowly slumping to being suddenly pole-axed), followed by lying prone (from a few minutes to many hours). Then there is shaking (from mild trembling to violent jerking) and movement of the whole body (from 'pogo' jumping on the spot to leaping about). Others have emotional outbursts of weeping or, more commonly, laughing (from giggling to raucous guffaws). Strangest of all are the 'animal' noises (which can sound like a roaring lion or even mooing cows and clucking chickens).

The spectrum of these activities covers the range from voluntary to involuntary, conscious to unconscious. Some can be continued or stopped at will, others seem beyond control. It is possible both to encourage and to discourage such behaviour.

It is hardly surprising that all this should result in negative reactions, which have ranged from bewilderment to disgust. Often this response is more intuitional than rational – a gut feeling that there is something wrong somewhere.

Of course, there may be different explanations for this instinctive recoil. It could be *traditional*. Such behaviour may never have been seen before and come as something of a shock. The 'ritualism' of formalised worship has hardly prepared people for such spontaneous expressions of emotion. Laughing in church is still irreverent for many. So for some it may simply spring from resistance to change, an objection to the unfamiliar. As such, it is no more significant than reaction to the current habit of opening eyes for prayer (which is more 'biblical'!) and to shutting eyes for praise (which is not!). 'It's not what we're used to.' This may be the simple reason why some are shying away, but I don't believe it is the only one.

It could be *cultural*. I have long advocated the 'de-Greecing' of the Church! Our Western lifestyle is far more influenced by Greek than Hebrew culture (from architecture to sport, democracy to drama). Within the Church, even the Protestant Reformers were profoundly affected by Augustine's Platonism and Aquinas' Aristotelianism – which separated the spiritual from the physical, the soul from the body. Worship became inward rather than outward, an activity of the mind and heart, with minimum bodily expression. Aerobic activity may have been acceptable in the stadium, but not in the sanctuary, where hearts may be lifted up but not hands! Jumping for joy is not welcome, even if it happened in apostolic times (Acts 3:8). The reaction against so much more physical activity in meetings is understandable. I freely admit I am embarrassed by 'action' choruses! But we have not yet exhausted all the possibilities.

It could be *biblical*. I believe that many would be willing to overcome their traditional and cultural inhibitions if they could be shown that there is a thoroughly sound basis for such goings-on in God's Word. That is precisely how many 'evangelicals', including myself, overcame anti-Pentecostal instincts and become 'charismatics'.

This is the fundamental problem: people want to know if there is solid biblical ground for believing that it is God who is pushing people over or causing such unusual patterns of behaviour.

Calling these happenings 'manifestations' prejudges the issue and seems to close the discussion. This is a biblical word, used to describe the supernatural gifts of the Spirit (1 Corinthians 12:7). To use it of these physical phenomena is to suggest quite strongly that they can be classed with prophecy, tongues and healing. Some quite openly talk about 'manifestations of the Spirit'. Even more explicit phrases extend this claim. Falling to the ground is described as 'being slain in the Spirit', a ghastly description which should only be used in such cases as that of Ananias and Sapphira (Acts 5:1–11). 'Going down under the power of the Spirit' is an even stronger wording. Lying on the floor afterwards is labelled 'resting in the Spirit'.

Some have gone even further. I have heard a number of speakers call the phenomena 'signs' and classify them with the 'signs and wonders' with which the Lord promised to confirm the preaching of the Gospel (Mark 16:20). The implication is that laughing or falling are adequate substitutes for healings and exorcisms as visible evidence for the authenticity of our ministry (with the added advantage that they seem to be rather easier to reproduce on an impressive scale!).

Significantly, much of the language I have been describing is not found in the Bible and where it is, it seems to be used rather differently. When novel jargon has to be coined (as in the 'Toronto blessing' itself), that inevitably arouses the suspicion that it has been difficult to describe something in biblical terms, which must in turn raise the question: 'Is it biblical?'

Of course, it must be recognised that a concept may be

biblical in *content*, even if a biblical *label* cannot be found for it; for example, the 'Trinity'. But proving this requires much more careful investigation. We all know that the Bible can be used to prove anything, especially when we appeal to general sense rather than particular statements (see the next chapter for the right use of 'proof-texts').

One thing is clear: Scripture never encourages unquestioning acceptance of whatever is claimed to be of God. There are constant warnings against deception and exhortations to 'Test everything. Hold on to the good. Avoid every kind of evil' (1 Thessalonians 5:21).

Ministry
The other problem is focused by the word 'ministry'.

An invariable pattern has rapidly developed which strongly suggests that the normal way to be 'blessed' by God is to be prayed for, usually with the laying-on of hands, at the climax of a public meeting, or even a gathering arranged solely for this purpose.

So limited has the term become that I am frequently asked if I will leave time for 'ministry' after I have spoken. Whatever happened to the ministry of Word and sacraments?

We have already noted that the normal means of blessing someone, whether by God or man, is by word of mouth. Blessing is usually pronounced upon a person, but can surely also be prayed for on their behalf.

And prayer with the laying-on of hands is certainly scriptural, though it appears to have been for specific purposes – receiving the Spirit, healing the sick or setting someone apart for particular ministry. I cannot recall any instance of this action associated with general prayer for one another. In passing, it may be observed that one quivering hand in front of the face and the other in the small of the back is probably rather different from apostolic practice!

But these are secondary matters. The primary issue is whether this is the necessary or even the normal way to receive God's 'blessing' today. The implication is that it is 'channelled' from a person who has it to a person who hasn't. Apart from the obvious risk of the wrong spirit being thus transferred (laying on hands in exorcism is to be avoided), there is another possible danger.

We live in a dependency culture, in which many would rather have things done for them than by them: welfare is the responsibility of others. This mood has infected Christian circles. It is easier to receive 'deliverance' than to exercise discipline in respect of habitual sins, though the New Testament has no mention of this 'ministry' (there's the word again!) in relation to believers. They have been delivered and have the Lord's promise that he will not let them be tempted beyond what they can bear (1 Corinthians 10:13).

We could be heading for a new kind of 'sacerdotalism', the need for a 'priest' to mediate the grace of God to us. When I have taught in Roman Catholic countries and congregations I have noticed the eagerness with which my hearers crowded me afterwards with requests for my prayer or blessing. Initially I felt encouraged (even flattered) by such a ready response. Later I recognised it as a revised standard version of 'Bless me, father, for I have sinned' and began to encourage them to approach the throne of grace boldly for themselves, as is their privilege and responsibility in Christ (Hebrews 10:19–22).

Over the last few years this kind of response seems to have spread to Protestant, evangelical and particularly charismatic circles. In more and more meetings the emphasis is shifting from corporate to individual activity and need (note how many choruses are of the 'I, me, my' category, rather than 'we, us, our'). The invariable climax is to invite people forward to be 'prayed for' by a team of selected personnel. These may not be recognised, much less ordained, as 'priests' – but that is their function.

Of course we believe in the priesthood of all believers, so that anyone can act in this capacity toward another. And Scripture exhorts us to confess our sins to one another and to pray for one another.

What I am questioning is an encouragement of the idea that the 'blessing' of God is to be communicated this way. Already some are developing a habit (in a few cases it might even be called an addiction) of coming forward frequently to be prayed for and laid out, in order to repeat or maintain their experience. Desire for a 'top-up' can easily develop into the need for a regular 'fix'.

This is hardly likely to produce maturity. Surely we want to see more direct dependence on the Lord in our disciples. While there is meant to be healthy interdependence within the fellowship of the Spirit, this is no substitute for the exercise of personal faith in prayer.

Ministering manifestations

The problem is compounded when 'ministry' and 'manifestations' are brought together, as they invariably are in what have come to be called by some 'drinking meetings'. The one is seen to lead to the other and it would take considerable discernment not to assume that the purpose is to minister the manifestations. This is particularly the case where people are prayed for until they 'manifest', at which point 'ministry' ceases.

It would be almost impossible for the ordinary observer not to conclude that such 'manifestations' are an integral element in the blessing, indeed that they are proof that the blessing has been received. Furthermore, it would be assumed that it is necessary to submit to 'ministry' to experience them.

The downside of this conclusion is that without such manifestations there has not been a complete or full blessing. This leads some to an attempted co-operation, even simulation, while being ministered to. It leaves others in painful frustration, wondering if they have been blessed or not. Those ministering can also be misled into false assumptions about the effectiveness of their ministry.

These, then, are the main difficulties that are being felt in relation to the 'Toronto blessing'. As we have indicated, there could be a number of different reasons for hesitation. This book is only concerned with one. It is written for those who ask the question: 'How does all this fit in with God's revealed will in Scripture?'

For such, a satisfactory answer would probably remove

any other reservations or at least enable them to be seen in
quite a different light. I believe that many would change
their attitude if this basic issue could be settled.

So to the Bible we must now turn.

CHAPTER 2

Is this that?

O N T H E day of Pentecost Peter explained what was happening by referring to Scripture: 'This is that.' It was the fulfilment of a divine promise. God said he would do it: now he's done it.

Can we do the same? Are there Scriptures that could have led us to expect what is now being experienced? If so, there should be no problem in accepting it.

At this point we encounter some ambiguity in the arguments being used to advocate acceptance of the phenomena.

The question is raised as to whether we need scriptural warrant for everything we do or not. It is pointed out that many of our practices in worship, fellowship and ministry are without biblical precedent. As long as these are not incompatible with any biblical imperatives, they may be regarded as legitimate.

This may (or may not) be a valid argument for human activity, but it is surely an inadequate criterion for discerning what is claimed to be divine activity. That would mean that every 'prophecy' that does not contradict Scripture must be assumed to come from God!

Strangely, those who advance this line of reasoning often seize on any text that has even a superficial resemblance to current happenings in support of their case. At the same time, we are cautioned against reliance on using the Bible as a source of 'proof-texts'! The video 'Rumours of Revival' contains a classic case of this kind of double-talk. The anchorman first warns viewers not to depend on 'proof-texts', then proceeds to give four!

I believe we do need a sound biblical basis for anything we claim to be divine activity. At the very least we ought to be able to show that it is entirely compatible with the character and conduct of the God who has revealed himself through his people Israel and his Son Jesus, as recorded in the Old and New Testaments. We are on even firmer ground if we can find actual precedents there. Before we look for these, some ground rules must be laid down about 'correctly handling the word of truth' (2 Timothy 2:15), especially in relation to producing 'proof-texts'.

Proof-texts

The Bible *as a whole* is the proof-text. It is only since it was mistakenly divided into chapters and verses, all numbered, that the word 'text' has been transferred from the whole to the smallest part, enabling a single sentence to be wrested out of its place and used on its own. This bad practice invariably changes the meaning of the text so that it can then be used to communicate what was never intended. Truly, a text out of context becomes a pretext!

But it is quite wrong to react against this abuse by

swinging to the opposite extreme. To reject specific statements of Scripture in favour of general impressions is to open the door to subjective and sentimental interpretations which are equally misleading and dangerous (for example: if the God of the Bible is love, how could he send anyone to hell?).

The fact is that any attempt to establish a biblical basis for an ingredient of belief or behaviour *must* quote individual statements to demonstrate the point. Whether it is a valid use of a text depends on three conditions.

First, the text must be given its original meaning as intended by the writer and understood by the readers. This involves some knowledge of the words and grammar used, as well as any cultural overtones involved. Reliable commentaries make these available to the serious student.

Second, the text must be seen in its context. That is not just the 'paragraph', i.e. the verses before and after the verse quoted. It may be part of a longer context, but the book in which it occurs is the most important thing to consider. Even which Testament is significant (the old covenant is now obsolete; Hebrews 8:13).

Third, all other relevant texts must be taken into consideration. This may reveal apparent contradictions. For example, on the first occasion on which Jesus sent out his apostles he told them to take no money on their missions; later, he countermanded that order (Luke 10:4; 22:36). Modern missionaries debate which counsel to follow – to raise support or 'live by faith'. Such problems can usually be resolved by closer examination of the original text and context.

In relation to this discussion, I have heard one of Jesus' beatitudes quoted in support of current phenomena ('Blessed are you who weep now, for you will laugh'; Luke 6:21), while its companion verse is totally ignored ('Woe to you who laugh now, for you will mourn and weep'; Luke 6:25). Taken together, neither verse is really relevant to the present debate. Both are addressed to 'his disciples', to believers and not to unbelievers. Both contrast their present with their future experience, their lot in this life with that in the world to come. Both assume the norm to be persecution and unhappiness now, with popularity and happiness as signs of compromise! Jesus himself illustrated this (John 15:18–19; Hebrews 12:2). Taking up the cross daily and following him is no laughing matter.

With these three principles in mind, we can begin our study of Scripture. Perhaps the simplest starting point is to see if there are any actual precedents for what have come to be called 'manifestations' in either the Old or New Testaments. Did such things happen then?

Physical effects

Falling

There are many examples of people falling to the ground in the presence of God: Ezekiel, Paul and John among many others. For some, that settles the question, but we need to ask whether this was the same thing as today. The following differences should be noted.

To point out that they were invariably alone, fell on their faces rather than their backs and were without the benefit of catchers or carpets could be regarded as quibbling, but it is not entirely irrelevant.

More important, it was invariably an involuntary response to an overwhelming and awesome 'manifestation' of the first or second person of the Trinity in visible and/or audible form.

It is never associated with the Spirit and certainly never interpreted as his work. The only mention of his activity in this connection was to lift Ezekiel to his feet after he had fallen, since God had not finished dealing with him (Ezekiel 1:28; 2:1). Levitation *is* a manifestation of the Spirit!

So there is not even a hint that the Lord ever pushed anyone over or knocked them down. Of course, he was indirectly responsible by appearing to them as he did. But the vital point is that their collapse is everywhere presented as a human reaction rather than a divine action.

Trembling
Again, this is frequently mentioned in Scripture, mostly associated with the emotion of fear and the result of a direct encounter between sinful people and a holy God, a strong conviction of guilt and a realisation of deserved judgment. This 'holy fear' is encouraged as a continuing and appropriate element of godly living. We are to work out our salvation with fear and trembling for it is God who works in us (Philippians 2:12–13).

It is never associated with blessing! Nor is it ever attributed to the Holy Spirit, though convicting of sin, righteousness and judgment is certainly his work (John 16:8).

It is a reaction of the nervous system to shock or stress, at its simplest a sign of nervous tension (as seems to be the case with Paul in Corinth; 1 Corinthians 1:3).

Laughing

The word is certainly used in the Bible. The problem is that there are so many different kinds of laughter, of which we need to consider at least four:

Humorous. Basically, this is to be amused by the ridiculous. There is humour in the Bible. Jacob's discovery of the ugly sister on the first morning of his honeymoon (Genesis 29:25), Elijah's teasing the prophets of Baal that their god was in the bushes relieving himself (1 Kings 18:27; 'turned aside' is a euphemism), Jesus' picture of a man walking around with a floor-joist in his eye socket offering to remove tiny splinters from other people's (Matthew 7:4) are just a sample. Our 'Western' humour is rather too subtle to appreciate it. Many Middle Eastern jokes are about camels (which we describe as 'a horse designed by a committee'). A sense of humour can be a 'saving grace', particularly if we are humble enough to laugh at ourselves, for we can be ridiculously naive!

Happy. This is probably the healthiest form, an experience of sheer exuberance. It is often due to a radical change for the better in outward circumstances, as when the children of Israel came home after exile in Babylon (Psalm 126:2). But we must not identify laughter with joy, though it may be one symptom of it. The Bible uses 'joy' and 'rejoicing' far more times than 'laughter' and 'laughing'. One is commanded and therefore is consciously maintained; the other is neither.

Haughty. This is the laughter of scorn and contempt and would seem incompatible with Christian character. This may be the laughter which Jesus cursed (Luke 6:25), referring to those who mocked his mission. Perhaps this kind of laughter is only safe for God to indulge in (as he does in Psalm 2:4). It ridicules and humiliates others, so involves judgment.

Hysterical. This again is a nervous reaction to extreme stress, which can even be mixed with weeping. It is usually irrational, an inappropriate response to the situation. It is also uncontrollable and only stopped by administering a sudden shock (such as a slap in the face). I cannot recall any instance of this in the Bible.

Again, we notice no justification for using such a phrase as 'laughing in the Spirit', though some forms are obviously valid responses to divine actions which have reversed circumstances. Shared joy and happiness can occasion corporate laughter.

Always in Scripture there is a good reason to laugh. Helpless laughter without an adequate or appropriate cause is not found.

It is noticeable that God only humiliates people by making them an object of fun or ridicule in judgment (the outstanding example is his promised treatment of a disobedient people; Deuteronomy 28:37). This reminder is needed when meetings are tempted to find the antics of some being 'overcome' amusing.

Weeping

This is far more common than laughter in the Bible. The Psalms are full of tears (Psalm 56:8 refers to the practice of sending a small phial containing genuine tears to the bereaved as a token of sympathy). Jesus himself wept at the grave of Lazarus and over the city of Jerusalem (there is no record of this 'man of sorrows' laughing).

But weeping in itself does not carry any spiritual significance, apart from the reason for it and the result from it. It is 'godly sorrow' that leads to repentance (2 Corinthians 7:10), which Esau's tears did not exhibit (Hebrews 12:17).

Yet again, tears are not taken to be a manifestation of the Holy Spirit, though they may well be the response of the human spirit to his work. They may simply be the release of an emotional crisis.

Leaping

We have already referred to the cripple healed through Peter and John. He had a good reason to jump for joy – he'd asked for alms and was given legs (Acts 3:6–7)! I am reminded of an evangelist's answer to a Cambridge student's enquiry:

'Can Christians dance?'

'Some can and some can't!'

'I meant: may Christians dance?'

'Yes, if they have something to dance about.'

So there are examples of spontaneous physical celebration in the Bible. Jesus used dancing as a metaphor for his ministry (Luke 7:32) and commanded his followers to 'leap for joy' – when they were hated, ostracised and insulted (Luke 6:23)!

But it is difficult to find any precedent for the involuntary and prolonged jerking that has been nicknamed the 'Toronto twitch' and 'pogo-ing'. Such spasms affecting parts of the body or the whole of it must probably be seen as symptoms of nervous tension. There seems no biblical warrant for identifying them as the work of the Spirit.

Growling

I am using this word to cover all strange noises, whether they sound like animals or not.

Christians may groan when unable to express their feelings in prayer (Romans 8:23). Jesus 'snorted' like a horse (with impatience or disgust?) when facing the tomb of Lazarus (John 11:33,38; the Greek word is *embrimaomai*). Micah howled like a jackal and moaned like an owl over the state of his nation (Micah 1:8). Notice that in each case there was a reason, a real situation to which the noise is an appropriate response. In no case is it a response to God.

Would God cause human beings, made in his image and only a little lower than the angels, to sound or behave like animals? The answer is yes, but only in judgment, never in blessing. The classic case is Nebuchadnezzar (Daniel 4); he was given the mind of an animal and made to eat grass like cattle to cure his over-wheening pride.

Animal behaviour seems to be far more likely to be of demonic than of divine origin, as everyone involved in exorcism knows.

Some quite bizarre exegesis has sometimes been used

to justify such noises. For example, Amos 3:8 has been quoted: if God roars like a lion, so may we. Actually, the verse speaks metaphorically and may only be extending the illustration of verse 4. 1 Samuel 6:12 has been used to justify mooing like cows, on the grounds that we are now 'bearing' the ark for the Lord. Weird manipulation of Scripture usually indicates desperation in the absence of any unquestionable foundation.

Stripping

I have heard about only two or three cases of this form of abandon to impulse, and restraint has been imposed as soon as it was realised what was happening. But it is a possible result when people are encouraged to stop thinking about themselves, let themselves go and do whatever they then feel like doing (fortunately, not many leaders encourage this immoderation, but some 'Toronto' associates have done so).

Curiously enough, there are biblical examples of this, notably in the first two kings of Israel! Saul, after the Spirit came upon him to 'turn him into another man', responded by lying naked on the ground all day and all night (1 Samuel 19:24). So far I have not heard this quoted, but it certainly would be if the practice became widespread. David stripped to his underwear (a linen ephod) to dance before the returning ark (2 Samuel 6:14–23). I have heard this referred to, but in connection with his wife Michal's disgust at his behaviour; her punishment of barrenness has been quoted as a warning to those who look down on the 'Toronto' happenings! In neither case does

Scripture state that God led them to behave in this way. It seems to have been their own choice.

On other occasions, prophets stripped as an acted representation of future judgment on Israel when God would return her to the nakedness of the day she was born (Isaiah and Micah both spread their message in this way). Since the Fall, nudity has become a shame and a disgrace (Genesis 9:21–3) and will never be restored as it was in Eden (Genesis 2:25). God clothed Adam and Eve (Genesis 3:21). Modesty in dress is now the rule, both on earth (1 Timothy 2:9) and in heaven (Revelation 7:9).

Nakedness is associated with demonic possession as well as divine judgment. Proof that Jesus had delivered the Gadarene demoniac from his possession was that his neighbours found him 'dressed and in his right mind' (Mark 5:15). It seems hardly likely that Jesus would want anyone naked and out of their mind!

It is time to summarise our findings in this chapter.

At first sight, there would seem to be some biblical parallels to the physical and emotional phenomena occurring today. But a closer examination of the situation in which they occur and the significance attached to them revises first impressions.

None of them is specifically stated to be a 'manifestation' of the Spirit. They are therefore not directly caused by him or willed by him to happen.

They are clearly regarded as human reactions, spontaneous responses of human nature. It is therefore valid and necessary to ask what the person is responding to as well as how they are responding.

They are often responding to a powerful revelation of Father or Son. In this case, they are indirectly caused by the Lord, even if he did not 'make' them happen.

They are nowhere defined as 'signs' of God's presence or power. though they may be a consequence of such an encounter. They are not interpreted as confirmatory evidence of the truth of the Gospel.

These reactions are not confined to divine experience. They may also result from human or demonic stimulation, or simply from changed circumstances.

There is therefore a need for careful discernment and distinction when examining particular examples.

They are not normally expected or encouraged as a response to God (there are a few exceptions in commands to weep or leap). They should certainly never be forced, either in one's self or by others. Significantly, there is no record of any happening as the result of 'ministry', through prayer with the laying-on of hands.

Above all, they are rational responses. I do not mean that they are thought through in the mind before being acted out in the body. The reality of the response is its spontaneity. I do mean that there is an adequate cause for which the response is appropriate. Helpless laughter or weeping without a reason is unhealthy.

To finish on a positive note, genuine responses of an emotional or physical kind are faithfully recorded as such in Scripture. Hebrew language and culture are more open to this than typical Western Christianity. God seeks a response from the heart as well as the mind, the body as well as the soul and spirit. He wants the whole person.

So far we have only considered possible precedents for particular phenomena. There are other general features which deserve chapters of their own, among them what some have begun to describe as 'a theology of drunkenness'.

CHAPTER 3

These are not drunk

THE general demeanour of many who are being 'blessed' is not dissimilar to a state of inebriation – muddled minds, slurred speech and unsteady gait. This has led to such phrases as 'intoxicated with God' and 'drunk in the Spirit'. Sometimes an appeal is made to the word 'enthusiasm', which is derived from the Greek phrase *en theos* = in God (the secular twentieth-century equivalent is 'emotionalism').

It has become commonplace to claim that an experience of the Spirit can easily simulate drunken behaviour. Two verses in particular appear to give sound biblical warrant for this: Acts 2:13 and Ephesians 5:18. Both need very careful exegesis.

Acts 2:13

Onlookers on the day of Pentecost said that the 120 disciples of Jesus had 'had too much (sweet) wine'.

The argument goes that they must have appeared drunk to warrant this misunderstanding. Advocates do not hesitate to assume that they must have been laughing, staggering or even rolling about on the ground – though

Scripture actually mentions none of these things. 'Arguments from silence' are always tricky and can be used either way. We must not read into the Bible what is *not* there (eisegesis) but read out of it what *is* there (exegesis). Even if they were in such a state, Luke did not consider it significant enough to report it. He probably only included the accusation to explain the clever opening of the faithful record of Peter's sermon.

It is more important to note what is actually said.

It was the *sound* of what the disciples were saying, not the *sight* of what they were doing, that drew a large crowd together. Their only recorded activity was to be speaking all at once, which would multiply the volume. The only unusual observation of the crowd was their dress, indicating Galilean origin. They had neither heard the wind nor seen the tongues of flame, which would have produced fear rather than curiosity.

The crowd did not think they were drunk, since their speech was totally intelligible in content, indeed astonishingly so, considering that the speakers only had elementary education and yet were speaking many languages fluently. The general reaction was amazement rather than contempt.

But every crowd contains a few sceptics ('some' indicates a minority). These were motivated by a desire to ridicule and mock the disciples, presumably because they were uneducated Galileans from 'up north'. Their comment is an attempted explanation rather than an accurate observation. Either they were not near enough or willing enough to listen to what was being said or they would not have had the courage to offer such a silly suggestion. Alcohol never yet produced linguistic ability!

Peter 'stood up' with the other eleven apostles (they must have been sitting or perhaps kneeling for the morning time of prayer in the temple, the 'house' of God; they certainly didn't rush out into the streets from an 'upper room', as evangelistic enthusiasts often portray the scene). He skilfully picked up the comment and effectively answered it (a useful technique for speakers – use your audience to make a point): 'it's only nine in the morning!' (Acts 2:15).

Having said all this, there must have been *some* similarity with drunkenness for the critics to have any hope of impressing others with their comment. The facts that we have provide a sufficient account. Over a hundred people engaged in uninhibited praise that could be heard throughout the building, everybody speaking but no one listening, with total lack of the co-ordinating language normally used by groups praying together in the temple – all this added up to a public disturbance at the hour of prayer which could easily be interpreted as an invasion of a party of drunks, especially by those who were motivated by a desire to ridicule. Paul later assumed that a congregation all speaking in tongues simultaneously, apart from anything else, could give an observer the impression that they were 'out of their minds' (1 Corinthians 14:23; see also the next chapter).

So the majority of Pentecostal observers were amazed at the mental competence of the disciples. Only a minority, for their own reasons, attempted a degrading accusation of incapability. Sceptics and cynics usually have blind-spots!

Ephesians 5:18

'Do not get drunk on wine, which leads to debauchery Instead, be filled with the Spirit.'

The argument goes that in using this conjunction of ex-hortations, Paul is making a *comparison*. The two states are similar in both experience to self and appearance to others. The difference between them lies in the *cause* of the state and its *effect*, the roots and the fruit. One enthusiastic advocate has even claimed that 'drunk' and 'filled' are virtually the same word or at least have the same conno-tation.

Actually, Paul is making a *contrast* rather than a com-parison. This is indicated by the word 'instead' and even more clearly by the immediate context. The whole chapter is emphasising that salvation must lead to a radically dif-ferent lifestyle. Believers must leave behind their former immorality, impurity, greed, obscure speech, etc. To con-tinue in this way will forfeit any inheritance in the king-dom of Christ and of God (Ephesians 5:5; cf. 1 Corinthians 6:9; Galatians 5:21). They must therefore be 'careful' and 'wise' – we would say 'circumspect' – in their behaviour.

Why, then, should Paul put this negative and this positive imperative together? The very word 'instead' im-plies a connection as well as a contrast between the two. The answer is that there are alternative ways of handling the same situation. When the old self is tempted to do one thing (get drunk), the new self should do another

'instead'. What makes people want to get blind drunk?
Usually great joy or sorrow, a desire to celebrate or com-
pensate. Paul is giving believers a new way of expressing
such pressures: 'be filled with the Spirit' or, literally, 'be
filled in Spirit'.

Most commentators point out that the verb is in the
present tense, which in Greek can mean a continuous act –
'go on being filled'. They usually go on to interpret this as
a continual state of sanctification, which robs this phrase
of its contextual meaning. The present tense can also be
translated as 'be being filled' and can therefore refer to
particular occasions.

The usual time for Christians to seek such convivial
company with each other would be in the evening, after
the day's work. This provides a further explanation for the
conjunction of alcoholic inebriation and spiritual celebration in the same sentence. Both are most likely to happen
at the same time (1 Thessalonians 5:7; compare Acts 2:15).
How Christians behave at night is just as important as
how they conduct themselves during the day.

That we are interpreting this along the right lines is confirmed by the named result of being 'filled'. In the original
language verses 19 and 20 are one continuous sentence
with verse 18. 'Speak' and 'sing' are adverbs rather than
verbs ('speaking' and 'singing'). Whereas drunks talk and
sing to themselves, here it is 'to one another', and
therefore is totally intelligible. So the Spirit-filling in this
context leads to mutual edification rather than personal
sanctification. It is obviously impossible to engage in such
activity continuously throughout life but it can and ought

to be enjoyed regularly. '*Always* giving thanks' means on every such occasion.

By contrast, bouts of drunkenness lead to 'debauchery', a word combining notions of loss of self-control, dissolute behaviour, profligate spending and offence, even harm, to others. It is not surprising that throughout the Bible, drunkenness is condemned as sinful and degrading, though moderate drinking is accepted (Psalm 104:15; it is highly unlikely that this refers to unfermented grape juice!).

In view of the fact that the loss of self-control is the prime result of drunkenness, it would be astonishing if the Spirit were to lead us into a simulation of this, particularly in the light of the apostolic imperative to avoid all appearance of evil (1 Thessalonians 5:22).

There are more direct references to be considered. One flavour in the fruit (singular) of the Spirit is self-control (Galatians 5:23). God has 'given us a spirit of power, of love and of calm and well-balanced mind and self-control' (2 Timothy 1:7; Amplified Version). In his 'pastoral' epistles, Paul commands that both men and women, old and young, need to be taught to be self-controlled, one element of which is not to be addicted to too much wine (Titus 2:1–6). There are also frequent calls in the New Testament for a life of sobriety (1 Thessalonians 5:6,8; 1 Peter 1:13; 4:7; 5:8).

In fact, there is no suggestion that those in whom the Spirit moves lose control of themselves. There may be spontaneous expression, but it is never involuntary. The Holy Spirit never *makes* us do anything. His anointing and gifting are under our control.

Corporate behaviour

It is especially important to remember these things when believers meet together. There are different guidelines for individual and corporate behaviour. Uninhibited worship in the privacy of one's own home is not necessarily acceptable in church. For example, in private Paul spoke aloud in tongues more than any, or even 'all', of the Corinthians; yet in public services he chose to use only intelligible language (1 Corinthians 14:18–19).

This fourteenth chapter of Paul's letter to Corinth is the 'locus classicus' ('most authoritative passage on a subject' according to the *Oxford English Dictionary*) on behaviour in public meetings of the church. It was written because the Corinthian meetings had too much of the Spirit's activity! Surely no one can have too much? Yes, it is possible – to have too many prophecies, too many tongues, for example, even though all are inspired by the Spirit. Paul is not here dealing with counterfeit or imitation, but with the genuine article.

Four basic principles applying to the conduct of public worship and fellowship emerge from this chapter.

1. The control of the meeting is a human responsibility. We can go further and say that the moving of the Spirit is in our hands. He may give the gifts, but their 'manifestation' is up to us. 'The spirits of prophets are subject to the control of prophets' (v. 32). A message may be given to a prophet but it doesn't *have* to be given to the people, if another has also received a message. A tongue may be given, but it shouldn't be spoken aloud unless an interpreter is present. Spiritual gifts can and must be controlled or use

turns into abuse. It is not that we are being told to control
the Spirit, but that we are to control our spirits, through
whom he works. We are therefore held responsible for
what he does in a meeting! True, we can quench the Spirit
by not allowing him to do anything, but we must not
swing to the opposite extreme of allowing, much less encouraging, anything and everything to happen. 'Let go of
yourself and let the Spirit do whatever he wants' is hardly
in line with Paul's teaching.

2. When Christians gather together, the prime purpose
is mutual edification rather than individual expression.
The first concern is not what *I* feel like doing, but what will
most help those around me to engage in meaningful worship. Worship leaders who exhort each worshipper to 'do
their own thing' (sit, stand, kneel, dance, etc.) are, in fact,
encouraging private rather than public worship. We need
to consider the impression we are giving to others, especially those Paul labels as 'outsiders' (not yet Christians)
and 'beginners' (only just Christians). We need to be particularly sensitive about anything that would confuse or
discourage either group. If Paul thought that simultane-
ous use of tongues by the whole congregation would con-
vey an impression of being 'out of your mind' (v. 23), one
wonders what his comment on contemporary 'manifestations', including helpless laughter and jerking, would
have been!

3. We can only edify others through their understanding. This could be called the principle of intelligibility.
Paul put strict limits on the use of tongues in public for this
very reason. One at a time, two or three at most, every one

to be interpreted (i.e. translated into common speech) –
these were his rules for using this gift in public. Only
through shared understanding can proper prayer and
praise be offered to the Lord (v. 16). In private, both prayer
and praise may be of the spirit without the mind (v. 15).
But public worship needs a harmony of mind and spirit.
Only that which communicates a clear content to others
will edify them (v. 8). Unusual physical activity may en-
tertain or even impress, but it is not likely to edify, in the
biblical meaning of that word.

4. Our meetings must reflect and represent the nature of
God. This can be put another way: our worship must
honour his name. Uppermost in our minds must be the
knowledge that 'God is not a God of disorder (confusion)
but of peace (harmony)'. This is not communicated when
everybody is 'doing their own thing' or when many different things are happening at once. There is need for an
'order' of worship. That does not mean formality. Flexibil-
ity is also necessary. Form and freedom are both needed in
public meetings. The right balance will encourage individual participation – for the common good, the benefit of
everybody else. And all must demonstrate that God
brings order out of chaos. That is why 'everything should
be done in a fitting and orderly way' (v. 40).

It is significant that all four principles are given in the
context of the Holy Spirit's activities in the Corinthian
meetings, rather than with reference to cases of human
misbehaviour on such occasions (for example, getting
drunk at the Lord's Supper; 1 Corinthians 11:21). It is precisely when the Spirit is moving most that our responsibil-

ity for controlling what happens is most tested and most needed. There is no biblical warrant for 'handing over the control of the meeting to the Holy Spirit'. That is an abdication of responsibility.

In this chapter we have looked at some practical aspects of our enquiry. We must now consider some doctrinal implications.

CHAPTER 4

The Bible says

THE branch of biblical theology dealing with the person and work of the Holy Spirit is called 'Pneumatology' (from the Greek word *pneuma*, which means wind, breath or spirit). There is a great deal of material, particularly in the New Testament, with which to build a 'systematic' understanding of his activity. We have a detailed record of what he has done in, for and through people. And there is a remarkably rich vocabulary to describe this.

The question arises as to how and where contemporary happenings fit into the biblical scheme of things. To answer this we need first some kind of classification of the Spirit's activity in the early church which we can use in identification of his movements today.

I propose a simple threefold grouping which I believe to be both comprehensive and consistent as far as the biblical record goes. The work of the Spirit may be classified as initial, special and continual.

Initial
I am using this term to describe the beginning of a person's experience of salvation.

The process of being born again is, of course, the work of the Holy Spirit from first to last. But a vital step is the conscious reception of the Spirit, without which initiation into the life of the kingdom is incomplete (repentance, faith and baptism are the other vital components; see my book: *The Normal Christian Birth*, Hodder and Stoughton , 1989).

Many words are used to describe this initial encounter with the Spirit. The simplest is 'received' (for he is a gift). Other synonyms include 'baptised in', 'filled with', 'anointed with' and 'sealed with'. It is also said that the Spirit has 'fallen upon' or been 'poured out on' the recipients.

Clearly, this is a rich experience which can be regarded from different viewpoints and described with a varied vocabulary. Clearly, it is also a conscious experience, so that recipients know it (Acts 19:2; Galatians 3:2), as well as any present at the time (Acts 8:18; 10:47).

So what happened when the Spirit was received? What audible or visible phenomena accompanied the gift?

On the very first occasion wind was heard and fire seen, but these were not seen by onlookers and appear not to have been repeated. One of the signs did continue – speaking unlearned languages, or 'tongues'. In addition, spontaneous praise and prophecy in native language accompanied the tongues (Acts 10:46; 19:6).

Thus, inspired speech is the only recorded effect of receiving the Spirit. The language may or may not be recognised, but it is clearly a language intelligible to someone (note 'of men and of angels' in 1 Corinthians 13:1).

It is significant that no other physical actions or reactions are mentioned as outward evidence. That some form of spontaneous speech is everywhere alluded to is in keeping with the Old and New Testament concepts of the Holy Spirit as primarily the Spirit of prophecy, whose presence is most likely to be indicated by some sort of 'prophesying' with the mouth.

In passing, we note that the Spirit is often received through prayer with the laying-on of hands, but this is by no means always so.

Special

Of all the verbs used to describe the initial encounter, only one is repeated on later occasions of empowering in the same people – namely, 'filled'. Those who were filled on the day of Pentecost were filled again a short time after (Acts 2:4; 4:31).

It would seem that the modern habit of referring to repeated 'anointings' is not, strictly speaking, the scriptural use of the term. For the early believers, their 'anointing' had been received once and for all at their conversion (1 John 2:27). But it is valid to speak of repeated 'fillings'.

These experiences were given for specific needs in particular situations, usually critical circumstances in which the Gospel needed to be preached but where opposition was intense.

As with the initial encounter, the only result in those so 'filled' was speech, particularly a courageous outspokenness (see Acts 4:8,31; 13:9). This pattern of being filled with the Holy Spirit in order to speak out the words of

God may be traced back through Zechariah, father of
John the baptiser (Luke 1:67) to the Hebrew prophets (e.g.
Micah 3:8).

Every such special 'filling' issued in speech of some
kind. No other physical effect on those filled is mentioned,
though on one occasion the building in which they met
was shaken (a sure sign of God's power and presence!).
Even the exhortation we have already considered in the
last chapter (Ephesians 5:18) urges readers to seek a filling
in order to speak and sing to one another.

Such 'fillings' come direct from God, usually in answer
to prayer. There is no case for seeking a renewed filling
through 'ministry' from someone else. Laying-on of hands
appears to be confined to initiation (Hebrews 6:2).

Continual
The Holy Spirit is given to abide (stay, remain, reside) in us
(John 14:16). His ongoing work is twofold, equipping us
for service to others and enabling us for sanctification in
ourselves. His gifts are for one and his fruit for the other.

Gifts for service
These are not given to enrich our own spiritual experience
(with the partial exception of tongues). They are supernatural abilities to evangelise and edify others.

Most of them are gifts of speech (words of wisdom,
knowledge, prophecy, interpretation). Some make possible supernatural deeds (miracle, healing).

They may be received through the laying-on of hands (1
Timothy 4:14; 2 Timothy 1:6; there is a question whether

these refer to the same occasion). This is usually in connection with a specific office or ministry in the church. There is no hint that further 'anointings' or 'fillings' are necessary for each use of the gift, but they can fall into disuse by neglect and need to be stirred up again. All exercise of gifts requires faith.

As we saw in the last chapter, such gifts are entrusted to the recipient as regards their use, or abuse. They can be divisive and even dangerous when exercised without true love (1 Corinthians 13).

Fruit for sanctification

The word is singular, one fruit with nine flavours (Galatians 5:22–3). Three relate us properly to God (love, joy, peace); three relate us properly to others (patience, kindness, goodness); and three relate us properly to ourselves (faithfulness, meekness, self-control).

All nine are clearly seen in Jesus himself. The fruit of the Spirit is the reproduction of his character in us. A few 'flavours' may be found in unbelievers, since no one in this life has altogether lost the image of God. Believers, inhabited by the Spirit of Christ, will exhibit all nine 'flavours' simultaneously; though it needs to be pointed out that fruit takes time to develop and ripen and this process can be retarded, even suspended.

The fruit of the Spirit grows as a result of 'walking' in the Spirit as 'led' by the Spirit – and by not walking after the 'flesh' (our old sinful nature, rather than the physical body).

Spiritual maturity is usually described in the New Testament as being 'full' of the Spirit rather than being 'filled' (Acts 6:3–5), though the term may include gifts as well as fruit, power as well as purity (Acts 6:8).

With this brief summary in our minds, we can ask where the 'Toronto blessing' fits in. Which of the three phases, or aspects, of the Spirit's activity are we witnessing?

To focus the enquiry, we are asking what has happened, *according to the Scriptures*, when someone has been 'ministered' to and exhibited 'manifestations' (whether falling, laughing, jerking or whatever).

Have they 'received' the *initial* gift of the Spirit for the first time? Can we think of this as their 'baptism' in the Spirit? Are they now 'sealed' and 'anointed'?

Or has this been a *special* 'filling', whose primary purpose is to embolden them to preach the Gospel and witness to their faith?

Or is it part of the *continual* work of the Spirit in their lives, with a view to producing gifts for others and fruit in themselves?

Could it be any one of these three and can we only identify which in each individual case? Or could it be none of these and something else altogether?

To the pragmatist, such questions are an irrelevant distraction. Who cares what it is as long as people are getting 'blessed'?

For conscientious preachers and teachers, life is not so simple. Called to declare the whole counsel of God, they have to wrestle with these issues in order to communicate God's promised blessings with clarity and confidence.

They must exhort their hearers to appropriate these and instruct them clearly how to do so. But they need to have the authority of Word and Spirit to be effective. People can only be expected to reach out in faith for what comes to their ears and hearts with this dual authority

In my Preface I have confessed my own dilemma in this regard. I have thus far found it difficult, if not impossible, to say with Peter: 'This is that', directing attention to relevant scriptural promises.

I suspect, therefore, that the issue has been clouded in some way, which would explain the uncertainty and bewilderment I have encountered in others. Can we identify a root cause of the confusion?

I believe we can locate it in the custom of referring to human reactions as 'manifestations' of the Spirit. The physical phenomena may be genuine responses to the power and presence of God but it is misleading to attribute them to the work of the Spirit.

This identification is compounded by two other growing habits of speech relating to 'ministry' times.

Invocation of the Spirit
The first is the 'invocation' of the Spirit, the practice of inviting and welcoming him to the gathering. John Wimber did much to encourage this, though some hymns had already set a precedent.

Apart from the fact that this is often done towards the end of a meeting (with the inference that he has not been present until then!), the practice is dubious from three points of view:

First, it reinforces the association of subsequent events with his 'coming'. If nothing happens, there will be disappointment, perhaps guilt. If anything happens, it will be assumed to be all of the Spirit.

Second, it overlooks the fact that the Spirit has been present all along precisely because he already indwells those who have received him. He does not need to 'come' to those in whom he already resides! Those who have met together are already 'the temple of the Holy Spirit' (1 Corinthians 6:19).

Third, and most important, there is no biblical precedent for praying *to* the Spirit, only *in* the Spirit. He was never directly addressed in this way by the early church. Why not, since he is the divine third person of the Trinity?

Father and Son are both kings, sitting on thrones and wearing crowns. None of this is ascribed to the Spirit, whose function is to bring us under the authority of the other two. Petitions in any 'kingdom' are addressed to the throne (Hebrews 4:16).

That is why the Spirit is rarely the subject of a verb in the New Testament. He does not give himself or pour himself out. He is the medium, not the agent, in Spirit-baptism (1 Corinthians 12:13; 'by' is a mistranslation, the Greek is 'in'). On the day of Pentecost, Peter was careful to say: 'Exalted to the right hand of God, he (Jesus) has received from the Father the promised Holy Spirit and has poured out what you now see and hear' (Acts 2:33).

This is not a quibble, a quaint example of pedantic semantics! The way we talk is the way we think and the way we will lead others to think.

'Drinking' meetings

The second way in which attributing 'manifestations' to the Spirit is reinforced is the use of the term *drinking* meetings' to describe Toronto-style gatherings. This word is very much associated with the Holy Spirit in the New Testament, as are other liquid metaphors (baptised, poured out).

While 'drink' is sometimes in the aorist tense, referring to the single occasion of initiation (e.g. in 1 Corinthians 12:13; where it is equivalent to baptism in Spirit), it usually refers to persistent practice (in John 7:37 the verb is a 'continuous present' imperative, meaning 'go on drinking'). To the woman at the well in Samaria, as well as in the temple at Jerusalem, Jesus described the Spirit as a never-failing spring producing constantly flowing streams of 'living water' (John 4:14; 7:38).

But is it right to apply the term, or the concept, of 'drinking' to meetings where people are being prayed for? Is this what Jesus meant?

More than one person has said to me: 'If you want a good response nowadays ask anyone who is thirsty to come forward'! But is it right to use such language at all in these circumstances?

Apart from giving both 'ministry' and 'manifestations' a 'pneumatological' connotation, this kind of talk overlooks one essential element in Jesus' teaching – that the spring of living water would be within the person themselves, the streams flow 'out from the innermost being' (John 7:38; Amplified Version). If this is the case, it appears incongruous to seek 'ministry' from someone else in order to have a 'drink'. That's more like asking someone else to drop a bucket in the well for you than being refreshed by your own inbuilt spring.

This idea of 'drinking' is also likely to lead to repeated returns to the well for more! Those who have been 'blessed' once have a strong incentive to come back again.

Perhaps what we should be doing is teaching people to drink from their own springs, which can be done at any time or place and does not require the help of anyone else. This seems the more biblical way of refreshment.

'Refreshing' is another term that has gained prominence in the current vocabulary, together with a renewed emphasis on 'revival'. We must now look at these words in the light of Scripture.

CHAPTER 5

'Revival' and 'refreshing'

AMERICAN Christians I have spoken to have not hesi-
tated to refer to the current move as the 'Toronto revival'. Typically, British Christians have been a little more
reserved and prefer the word 'refreshing'. Both need to be
examined.

Revival

To begin with 'revival', the first question relates to its
meaning. While many talk about it and pray for it, few dis-
cuss a definition. Most are content to refer to historical
events with a feeling of nostalgia ('Lord, do it again'). The
most recent reference point is the Hebridean revival,
closely followed by the Welsh one, with 1859 and 1740
representing the previous two centuries. The concept is
historical rather than biblical.

What people expect when 'it' comes also varies. Some
focus on a revitalised Church. Others see a great increase
in the results of evangelism. A few expect the world to experience spontaneous conviction. There is even a hope
that it would enable the Church to take over the world.

No one could argue against the need of the Western

churches for a transfusion of new life (and new blood!). As society becomes increasingly secularised, as cults and sects abound, as vice and crime flourish, as family life disappears – Christians feel increasingly helpless to stop the rot and reverse the trends. At its simplest, the prayer for revival is born of a recognition that only God's direct intervention could change the situation.

No wonder, then, that many look back with nostalgia to notable periods of advance and long for a repetition. The very word *re*vive carries this backward reference. The Church *has* seen periods of intensified spirituality but they have often been quite brief and difficult to sustain.

This raises the question as to whether a state of 'revival' is normal or abnormal, whether such intensity is a temporary shot in the arm or meant to be the permanent pattern of church life. We know that the *average* picture is well below such times (and has been for most of church history); but what should be *normal*?

An even more fundamental question is: Why are we not in revival? Who is responsible for holding it back? There are two quite different answers (which relate somewhat to the 'Calvinist' and 'Arminian' understandings of God's will).

One finds the answer in God's sovereignty. The decision is entirely his. He will send revival when he wants to and chooses to. Mind you, many holding this view pray for revival, believing this can affect his programme (perhaps he has decreed that when there is a sufficient quality and quantity of prayer, he will send revival).

The other finds the answer in man's responsibility. It is

our failure to co-operate that holds up the moving of God's Spirit. In Christ we already have all the resources we need to build the Church and evangelise the world. Revival awaits our sincere repentance and total obedience.

Both groups seem able to pray together for revival, in spite of such different premises. They are driven together by the pathetic state of the Church and the tragic state of the nation.

Are their prayers being answered in what has stemmed from Toronto? Three opinions are emerging.

First, this is *not* revival. Compared to previous outbreaks it lacks many of the traditional hallmarks (for example, a large influx of new converts).

Second, this *is* revival. God is moving widely and powerfully. The scale and speed is consonant with former times, even if the mode is different.

Third, this could be the *beginning*, the precursor of revival (some would be more definite and claim it certainly is). Many believe that we are seeing the first drops of a cloudburst. Others are more cautious (the title of the 'Toronto' video is significantly *'Rumours* of Revival').

Behind all this discussion lies a much more fundamental question: Is 'revival' biblical? It is certainly to be found in history, but does Scripture talk in this way? I know that some will find even raising this offensive. The word and concept are so widely used that it is taken for granted that we have biblical warrant. But have we?

One strong advocate for 'revival' has candidly admitted that there is 'no biblical framework' for it (Wynne Lewis, in the first issue of the new Elim magazine *Joy*). That is going too far. There may be no support for the idea in the New Testament but there is quite a bit in the Old.

God's people Israel were constantly backsliding from their God-given calling, becoming as bad as, even worse than, their pagan neighbours. Sensitive souls cried out for restoration of their fortunes after God had in anger abandoned them to their just deserts. His patience and commitment to his covenant promises led to their repeated revival as a nation (and their survival as a people to this day).

It is highly significant that those who speak and write about revival invariably use language from the Hebrew Scriptures:

'Oh, that you would rend the heavens and come down!' (Isaiah 64:1).

'Will you not revive us again, that your people may rejoice in you' (Psalm 85:6).

'May your people be willing in the day of your power' (Psalm 110:3).

One might even say that Israel was in perpetual need of God's reviving grace.

However, two features of this general picture must never be overlooked.

The first is that repentance and reformation had to happen *before* they could be revived. The constant refrain of the prophets was 'if my people . . .' Revival tarried until Israel made the first move. Such verses as 2 Chronicles 7:14 and Malachi 3:10 (which have become so familiar in recent years) put the onus on the people. There are preconditions for God's blessing. The prophets seem to have taken an 'Arminian' view of revival!

The second is that the people in general had not received the Holy Spirit, who was only given to a minority of God's people and then not always on a permanent basis, but for the fulfilling of special tasks. The reason for their failure is obvious. They simply did not have the moral and spiritual resources to maintain the high standards set for them in the Mosaic law.

But there were prophetic predictions that one day the Spirit would be poured out on all God's people, regardless of age, sex or class (Joel 2:28–9), the fulfilment of a wish of Moses (Numbers 11:29). This would write the law on the desires of their hearts (Jeremiah 31:33–4; Ezekiel 36:27; 37:14).

Those promises have now been fulfilled. The resources have been supplied. The 'last days' have begun. The Spirit is being poured out on 'all flesh'.

This partly explains why the New Testament has little or nothing to say about the 'revival' of God's people. That kind of talk is now inappropriate.

But we need to probe more deeply. The fact that the concept of 'revival' is missing from the apostolic doctrine is not for the reason which most people assume.

It is frequently asserted that the New Testament does not mention 'revival' because 'the early church was living in revival, so didn't need to think or talk about, much less pray for it'.

Such a trite statement needs very careful unpacking. The New Testament covers church history for about seventy years (some scholars would say more, others less). Did the 'revival' last this long? Many are thinking only of the earliest years, when thousands were being converted (from people prepared for centuries).

Certainly they experienced the guidance and dynamic of the Holy Spirit; and they made an impact on society. But it is very easy to idealise the early church, even idolise! A careful reading of the epistles reveals a more mundane picture.

If the Corinthian church was 'living in revival', few who pray for revival today would want to join a church like that. Would anyone claim that the Galatian or Colossian churches were in revival, or the fellowship to which Jude wrote? And what about the seven churches of Asia?

So what did the New Testament churches have that we haven't? They had most of the problems we have! If they hadn't had these, our New Testament would be a much slimmer volume! In fact, the more I study them, the more I see church life as it is around the world today.

The fact is that even within the apostolic period there was serious decline in both belief and behaviour, battles with false teaching and immoral living. Even the ascended Jesus threatened to close some churches down. So the notion that all the early churches lived in a permanent state of revival is a myth that needs to be exposed.

In spite of all this, the New Testament does not even mention the idea of revival, even to those churches in serious decline. There must be some other reason for this contrast with the Old Testament.

It could be the post-Pentecost advantage of the church over Israel. The power is now available to all and has not been withdrawn. The responsibility for lean years is no longer on God's side, but is now firmly laid at the churches' door – for not using the available resources. Israel had to wait for God to move; the Church does not have to wait.

It is striking that New Testament churches at a low ebb are called to repent and reform themselves rather than call on God to revive them. Compromise and complacency are the real obstacles. 'Repent or be removed' is what the Spirit says to churches that are in trouble.

Refreshing

What, then, of Peter's mention of 'seasons of refreshing' (Acts 3:19)? This is the nearest, perhaps the only, text in the New Testament that could be understood to indicate special times of divine visitation. It is widely used to describe current events, perhaps because 'refreshing' avoids the full-blown traditional understanding of 'revival'.

We must note the context. Peter is speaking to unbelieving Jews. He is urging them to *repent* and turn to God. This action on their part will make two things possible – 'seasons of refreshing' and the coming of their Messiah (Christ), who has already been killed by them (Jesus). Quite clearly, the second result refers to the second coming, the parousia.

But what are the 'seasons of refreshing'? The problem is that Peter does not define them in any way, leaving the way open to apply them to anything we choose!

In seeking to understand what he was referring to, we need to assume that his words made sense to his Jewish listeners. In the immediate context Peter refers to divine promises made long ago through his holy prophets. The coming of their Messiah is certainly from this source, so we may assume that 'seasons of refreshing' is also defined here and a familiar concept.

The word 'refreshing' itself is of interest. Its only occurrence in the Greek Old Testament is in Exodus 8:15, where it means *respite*, in this case from God's judgments. Though the word itself is not used by the prophets, the concept is widespread. Repentance brings forgiveness and relief from punishment. The use of the term in the New Testament is consistent with the idea of bringing relief from suffering (e.g. 2 Timothy 1:16).

This meaning perfectly fits Peter's sermon. Having established his hearers' guilt in disowning the Holy and Righteous One and killing the author of life, he offers them the hope of their just punishment being turned away and their rejected Messiah returning to them, leading to their centuries-old dream of the dawning of a new age, bringing relief and restoration. This dual promise, however, is dependent on their true repentance and the wiping out of their sins.

Peter is careful not to offer a permanent state of relief, since Jesus never promised such in this world (cf. Acts 14:22). But they will enjoy 'seasons' or 'times' of relief (he uses the word *kairos*, which refers to 'moments' of critical import, rather than *chronos*, duration time best translated as 'periods'.

Alas, the Jewish nation as a whole did not repent and there were only a few years' delay in God's judgment on them in the fall of Jerusalem in AD 70. Perhaps even this short time of respite was due to the fact that so many of them did repent and formed the early church.

But it is highly unlikely that Peter was referring to later (centuries later) periods of sudden advance in church history, however apt the phrase may be when taken out of context. Even if it were a valid application, Peter's point is that repentance must precede such seasons. The modern notion that revival is needed to produce repentance is alien to this Scripture. The danger of using this phrase to describe contemporary events is to give them a 'biblical' aura without an adequate authority.

Some have built on Peter's conjunction of times of refreshing and the return of Christ an expectancy that such refreshing will reach a climax just before his return. We must now look at this teaching on an 'end-time revival', which is now widespread.

CHAPTER 6

The end is in sight

ONE OF the usual features of a genuine move of the Spirit is an intensified expectancy of the return of our Lord Jesus Christ to planet earth. The ancient prayer of the Church 'Maranatha' (Lord, come!) springs readily to the lips, expressing a longing in the heart.

This is hardly surprising since Jesus sent the Spirit to take his place on earth and the Spirit must be looking forward to working with him again down here, as they did during his former ministry.

However, in recent years this 'blessed hope' has been strangely confused.

On the one hand, there has been a strong emphasis on 'the end-times', a sense of living at the conclusion of human history. Some have gone so far as to say that we are the final generation. This feeling has been fostered by the direction and speed of world events, coupled with the near completion of the second millennium AD.

On the other hand, there has been a diminished emphasis on the second coming. In the flood of new songs, hardly any refer to this event which is mentioned over three hundred times in the New Testament. Few sermons are addressed to this theme.

How do we explain this anomaly?

There has, in fact, been a massive switch from the traditional 'eschatology' (study of the 'last things', from the Greek word for 'end' = *eschaton*), which concentrated on what will happen *after* his return (the millennium, the day of judgment, heaven and hell) to an almost exclusive attention on what may happen *before* his return. The focus of Christian hope has radically changed.

This has happened over the last few decades. It has been encouraged by the use of the three R's – 'Restoration', 'Revival', 'Reconstruction'.

While there are differences between the views associated with these three words, they tend to share a common basic expectation. That is that the 'end-time' church will be the best yet, surpassing all previous phases of church history – not only in itself but in impact on the world. This hope engenders a mood of optimism, even triumphalism.

'Restoration' was first in the field, at least in this country. Teaching that the Church would establish the kingdom of God in this age, it encouraged many Christians to transfer from old denominations to new fellowships to be sure of being part of this 'kingdom' about to be 'established'. It has now become apparent that this hope is not much nearer fulfilment and disappointed people are looking in another direction.

'Reconstruction' has only reached a limited number of groups in this country but is now quite strong in America. It is a unique blend of Presbyterian and charismatic elements and believes the Church will be able to take over society and impose biblical laws, restoring morality. It is sometimes known as 'Dominion' theology. In Europe it appears naively optimistic.

'Revival' has become the dominant word in Britain. The obvious failure of both 'renewal' and 'restoration' to halt the decline of both Church and state has led to the feeling that only God can reverse the trend by sovereign intervention. The longing for this has met up with the teaching of an 'end-time revival', which had been gradually permeating fellowships through speaking, singing and writing.

All three R's, as we have said, tend to share an optimistic view of the immediate future. In theological terms, they incline to the 'post-millennial' position. That is, they expect to see Christ's rule on this earth to be established *before* Christ's return rather than *after* (i.e. his return will be 'post-millennial').

This expectancy of an 'end-time revival' produces an eagerness to see some evidence of its approach. Successive movements originating across the Atlantic have aroused intense interest here – 'Is *this* IT?' John Wimber's signs and wonders, Peter Wagner's territorial spirits, Paul Cain's predictions and now Rodney Howard-Browne's meetings – these have all been considered candidates for the 'big thing'. Most conclude that they have been staging-posts on the way.

Few seem inclined to ask the basic question: Has God promised an 'end-time revival'? Certainly there have been many 'prophecies' to this effect, but do they line up with Scripture (the first test of all prophetic claims)?

Again it may be significant that most appeals to a biblical basis turn to the Old Testament (as was also true for the general concept of revival). Two such references stand out.

There is an allegorical interpretation of God's promise of 'latter rain' to Israel. This is a meteorological phenomenon (spring rains that swell the grain for harvest before the annual six months' drought). Whether it can legitimately be understood as an eschatological prediction is a moot point.

The main appeal is to Joel's promise of a wide outpouring of the Spirit 'in those days' (Joel 2:29), which is taken to mean the end of time. It is linked to restoring the fortunes of Judah and Jerusalem (3:1), though few end-time revivalists make a point of this.

The test of our interpretations of the Old Testament must always be the New Testament. How, then, does apostolic doctrine confirm or deny this idea?

The first and most obvious thing to note is that the phrase 'last days' is taken to mean the whole of church history, not its final phase. For Peter the last days began at Pentecost and will finish at the Parousia (Jesus' return). For Paul too 'later times' (1 Timothy 4:1) had already begun, though he may well have considered that its characteristic trends would intensify.

However, there are some New Testament passages (e.g. in Thessalonians) and a major portion of one book (Revelation) which deal with events immediately preceding the return of Christ. Here, if anywhere, we would expect to see confirmation of a prophetic promise of an end-time revival. But there is not a trace of it!

Instead, we find the Church in Big Trouble, the 'Great Tribulation' (the grounds for believing that Christians will not escape this, except by martyrdom, may be found in my book: *When Jesus Returns*, Hodder and Stoughton, 1995). The world will be in the hands of an unholy trinity – the devil, the antichrist and the false prophet. Persecution will be at an all-time high.

Far from enjoying enormous growth, much less taking over the world, the Church is more likely to be reduced as '*many* will turn away from the faith and . . . the love of *most* will grow cold' (Matthew 24:10–12). The call is for endurance (Matthew 24:13; Revelation 14:12), to be faithful even to the point of death (Revelation 2:10).

The responsibility for preparing churches for tough times ahead is placed firmly on the churches themselves (Revelation 2–3). Having said that, we cannot believe that the Lord would not play his part by strengthening them by his Spirit. It would be reasonable (though this is speculation) to expect a 'move' of his Spirit to encourage the Church prior to a time of suffering.

If an 'end-time revival' did occur, it would more likely be a preparation of the church to be rejected by the world than to reign over it. The 'refreshing' would be for endurance rather than enjoyment, though that is probably not in the minds of those currently praying for it to happen.

CHAPTER 7

Good God

I BELIEVE that all our problems are at root theological and that we are all theologians. 'Theology' means simply how and what we think about God, whether we are intellectual or intuitive about it.

In relation to our subject, many find it difficult, if not impossible, to relate some of the more bizarre 'manifestations' to what they have come to believe God is like.

They find it unimaginable that God would want to make people fall about, laugh helplessly, make animal noises, suffer convulsions and generally lose control of themselves. That human beings, made in his image, just a little lower than the angels, should be treated by their Creator in such a way seems inconceivable, especially when it makes them the subject of amusement and even ridicule.

Others have problems relating it all to Jesus. Since he is the 'exact representation' of the invisible God (Hebrews 1:3) this is a valid exercise.

The fact is that there is no record whatsoever of any of these 'manifestations' resulting from his ministry to needy people. The very thought that when he 'blessed' the children, they crashed to the ground, seems preposterous.

Of course, we must recognise that our picture of Jesus is conditioned by many factors, some of which may be cultural rather than biblical. The 'gentle Jesus meek and mild' we sang about in Sunday School or the blue-eyed, fair-haired 'Scandinavian' pictured in children's Bibles may be very wide of the truth. The general image which many have is probably more sentimental than scriptural.

There is a tough side to his character. He 'lashed' people with tongue and whip. And we need to balance the Saviour of the gospels with the Judge of the Apocalypse, where he comes as a mass killer (Revelation 19:21).

But when all this is allowed for, there is still a gap between this Jesus and the things attributed to his Spirit today. We may try to close it by saying he is free to do whatever he wants to do, whether he has done it before or not. How then can we be sure that it is *he* who is responsible?

Let us return to the nature of God, since the Spirit is the Spirit of God as well as the Spirit of Christ.

Would God ever humiliate human beings? Would he ever reduce a man to the level of an animal?

The clear biblical answer is: Yes! He has already done this – notably in the case of Nebuchadnezzar (Daniel 4). He has sent evil spirits into people, with degrading results.

But, and it is an enormous 'But', he has only done this as a judicial act of punishment – for persistent pride or hardened hearts. Such 'signs' reveal his curse, never his blessing. He may do these things to sinners but not to saints.

This brings us to another issue – whether God would

ever choose to lead those whom he has redeemed into involuntary activity at all. Those who think that grace is an irresistible force might see it as a tribute to his power and sovereignty. Those who think of his grace as undeserved favour, freely given and freely received, are likely to see things differently.

Does God want to make us do things against our will? Or does he seek our active co-operation? Of course, some will point out that people do submit quite voluntarily to ministry, usually knowing perfectly well what may happen (the same knowledge may hold others back). But this leaves the question unanswered as to whether God wants us voluntarily to submit to involuntary actions which can be embarrassing to others if not ourselves.

Some justify it by saying that public humiliation is a divine test of our willingness to shed our pride (the same has been said about baptism by immersion, though it is extremely doubtful if that was a reason for the practice).

Certainly we need to be humbled, though most exhortations in Scripture are to humble ourselves (Matthew 18:4; James 4:10; 1 Peter 5:6). There is, however, a fine though important distinction between being humbled and being humiliated. The latter carries overtones of being degraded and despised. No wise parent humiliates a child, knowing what damage can result. Would the heavenly Father do otherwise?

So we are back to the original dilemma. Would the God we have come to know through Jesus resort to such devices to deal with our pride? Is this the way he would choose to humble his children or even, as some have daringly argued, glorify himself by mortifying us? Such reasoning seems to this writer closer to rationalisation than revelation.

The appeal to 'general impressions' of Scripture can be coloured by subjective presuppositions. Nevertheless, intuitive reactions of mature believers need to be taken seriously. I felt it necessary to articulate some of them in this chapter, though I do not consider them an essential element in my general thesis.

We must move on to a more compelling issue, which has been decisive for many. The desirable results seem to preclude any questioning of the methods used to achieve them. In a word, does not the end justify the means?

CHAPTER 8

By their fruit

FOR some, the contents of this book so far may appear somewhat superfluous, even irrelevant. They are quite prepared to admit that 'manifestations' and 'ministry' as experienced and practised today are without biblical parallel or precedent. They are often eager to point out that many other Christian activities are 'non-biblical' – like shutting one's eyes for prayer (more recently, opening them for prayer and shutting them for praise!), even having church buildings. In technical terms: is Scripture normative or regulative? Do we have to have a clear precedent or are things permissible that do not conflict with Scripture?

Perhaps the latter principle is adequate for *human* activities. But the former seems more appropriate for claims that *God* is doing something. If what he is said to be doing cannot be identified with his revealed activity recorded in Scripture, what reliable criterion can be used to detect his invisible presence?

At this point appeal is made to pragmatism (if it works it must be right) – a principle widely applied within some churches, particularly across the Atlantic, where 'success' is more highly regarded than here. However strange, even bizarre, the 'blessing' may appear at the time, this doesn't really matter as long as the later effects are good. Frequent appeal is made to Matthew 7:20: 'By their fruit you will recognise them.'

And there has been a flood of testimonies to continuing spiritual benefit from having been 'blessed'. There have been conversions and healings, though probably these are a minority of cases. More frequent are testimonies to deeper love for the Lord, greater freedom in worship, more desire to pray and boldness to witness. Prayer meetings have increased in numbers and length.

But does all this settle the issue? Does it prohibit questions?

How do we measure 'fruits'? How soon can we do so?

Perhaps we should be talking about 'results' rather than 'fruit', since the latter word is used of character as well as product. Since character takes time to develop and is only really seen under pressure, it would seem premature to judge the 'blessing' by this yardstick.

But we can 'judge' the results. It would seem that the majority of these are of an emotional nature – in a release from inhibitions that affects other areas of the Christian life by 'quickening' a desire for the things of God.

This is to be welcomed. For too long many Christians have been afraid of expressing emotions in public, a hang-up about letting feelings hang out. And, since emotions are usually expressed in a physical way, the inner inhibition has led to a reluctance to use the body more freely in worship. So a release from this handicap was needed in many churches – particularly, if I may dare say it, the established churches in our land, often so coldly formal. There is room for more joy and sorrow. As P. T. Forsyth put it: 'Our churches are full of the nicest, kindest people who have never known the despair of guilt or the breathless wonder of forgiveness'.

However, if this is to develop character, other dimensions of personality need to be changed. The mind and the will need to be touched, as well as the heart. Indeed, the Bible, while clearly accepting laughter and tears, puts much more emphasis on repentance (changed *mind*) and obedience (dedicated *will*) as the appropriate response to an encounter with the living God.

The ultimate test of any experience is whether it leads to real repentance and observable obedience. This yardstick is especially necessary in an age which is addicted to novel experiences and regards all religious experiences as self-authenticating. The Church must not fall into this way of thinking but faithfully 'test all things'.

In other words, the proof that a religious experience has been a genuine encounter with God is its effect in the two areas of belief and behaviour. That is because the Spirit of God shares the character of God and draws people into that likeness. He is the Spirit of truth and holiness.

Even if all these satisfactory 'ends' are attained, is the 'means' therefore entirely justified?

Quite bizarre evangelistic methods have sometimes been justified by the resulting conversions, however few. However, most would draw the line at immoral activity (an extreme example was the use of sexual favours to attract young people, as one deviant group of Christians is reputed to have done).

Clearly, the means must not contradict the end. If that end is godliness, ungodly means are counter-productive.

A 'grey' area is the offering of incentives of a different kind from the main objective. Missionaries have wrestled with the problem of encouraging acceptance of salvation by offering physical relief through food distribution or medical, surgical and educational facilities. This can produce 'rice Christians', as they were called. Jesus himself faced this dilemma (John 6:26).

Since these services are largely provided by public authorities in our situation, we are not so tempted to use welfare as a 'bribe'. But we could be in danger of offering emotional relief, an experience rather than the Gospel. I have come across young people simply wanting to be 'zapped'!

But we have strayed into another question: Does the end justify the *motive*? Does it matter why or what people are seeking, as long as they finish up with the right thing? However, this is only a variant of the main issue.

Neither the motive nor the method can be judged solely by results. Both must also be consistent with biblical instructions for ministry (e.g. as already outlined in chapter 3).

We must also ask what impression is left by the means used. That spiritual problems have a quick solution? That a regular 'pit-stop' on the floor will keep us topped-up in enthusiasm for the Lord? One of the disturbing aspects is the regularity with which some are already returning for another 'fix'.

We have already questioned this dependence on others. It is a feature of our age to want things done for us rather than to do things for ourselves. Deliverance is more congenial than discipline. A new kind of priesthood could develop. Some 'ministers' could get a name for being more able to channel the blessing than others. Conversely, ministries without this 'anointing' could be shunned.

In view of all these reservations, how can we explain the fact that many have testified to receiving 'blessing' through such 'ministry'? If God owns it, shouldn't we?

I believe the answer lies in God. He is full of mercy, slow to anger. He loves and longs to bless his creatures, animal and human (Genesis 1:22,28). It is his nature to bless us.

Nor does he wait until we are perfect before he blesses us. That is the essential wonder of justification. And he does not wait until our methods are perfect before he blesses our ministry, or which of us would he be using?

Because of this, it is a fundamental mistake to assume that his blessing ratifies our ministry in every respect. For example, his blessing on the dedicated service of the Salvation Army does not excuse their disobedience over baptism and the Lord's Supper.

Where people come in simple faith for his blessing, he will bless them, however weird their thinking about how the blessing is conveyed.

For example, there are cases in the New Testament of genuine healings through touching clothes (Jesus' shawl tassel, Paul's sweatband or even catching Peter's shadow). God honoured their faith – but there is no hint whatever that he wanted these means to be developed into regular ministries. Nor did the apostles show any signs of doing so! It was the medieval church which encouraged faith in saintly relics. The use of handkerchiefs has also reappeared in the modern church, even to communicate the 'blessing'.

It is a fine line between faith and superstition. Most superstitions are religious in origin. Even the sacraments may be treated superstitiously, when the focus is on the means or the minister rather than the Lord.

To be fair, 'Toronto' promoters have often endeavoured to focus attention on the Lord rather than themselves and on the inner encounter rather than the outer expression. However, the emphasis on 'ministry' has set up a conflict between words and deeds in this respect. The overall effect has been an emphasis on what happens, whether they like it or not.

And it has to be said that not all the results have been good. Some have 'manifested' without being 'blessed'. A few have been damaged through 'ministry' (I know of two who were crippled for weeks afterwards, but their subsequent instant release through a simple prayer revealed the condition as psychosomatic). There has been some division among fellow-believers, sometimes reaching the painful point of separation. A major concern is that unbelievers (perhaps more men than women) may be further alienated by what is happening. As one friend remarked to me: 'It seems strange if the Holy Spirit is calling us to mission and at the same time driving people away!'

At this stage it is difficult to quantify these negative effects, but they are happening and should not be quickly dismissed and disregarded on the ground that 'every campaign has its casualties'. The aim should be to keep these down to a minimum, as much as possible.

It is time to consider the practical application of our findings so far, especially in the conduct of meetings.

CHAPTER 9

Mainly for leaders

'N EVER finish a sermon without telling people exactly what you hope they'll *do* about it.' I was given that advice over forty years ago when I had just started preaching. I've never forgotten it, though I haven't always remembered it!

So what difference do I hope this book will make?

First, I hope it will make readers think, even think again, about the two questions of 'manifestations' and 'ministry'. Then I hope that there will be changes in the way our public gatherings are handled.

The basic issue raised was whether 'manifestations' are divine actions or human reactions. I believe the biblical answer is clear: they are never defined as the former and always described as the latter.

Once this is accepted, we can then go on to ask what place they should have in our meetings. I suggest the following guidelines.

1. *They will not be forbidden.* Readers may be surprised by my first conclusion after all I've already said! But I have nowhere said that human reactions are wrong. A genuine

response to God is surely a welcome thing. Nor should we exclude physical or emotional dimensions from that response. We are integrated creatures and need to express our whole being. The 'Greek' separation of body and soul has for too long inhibited and conditioned us to make only an inward, cerebral, 'spiritual' response. People need to learn again how to 'offer your *bodies* ... which is your spiritual worship' (Romans 12:1; noting that it goes on to talk about the renewing of the *mind* also).

2. *They will not be distracting.* There must be control in a corporate situation. Such individual reactions must not be allowed to distract others from necessary elements in public worship. The most obvious example is raucous laughter during preaching, which can detract from the hearing of the Word (the most notorious case I have heard of was during a sermon on hell!). Experience has shown that intrusive reactions *can* be controlled, especially when commanded to do so in the name of Jesus.

3. *They will not be encouraged.* It is one thing to allow them to happen; it is another thing to prepare for them to happen (carpets, catchers, cleared chairs). And yet another to build up an expectancy that they will happen. This road can lead to manipulation by the leaders and simulation by the led; the results are much less impressive than the real thing.

4. *They will not be publicised.* The temptation to put such things on display is very strong (especially when video cameras are around). If such responses are considered to validate the 'anointing' on a minister, the success of a meeting or the presence of God, there is considerable pres-

sure to have them happen as publicly as possible. Perhaps it would be safer to offer 'personal' ministry in an after-meeting or in another room. This would avoid the widespread impression that this is the *real* climax and purpose of the meeting, to which the worship and the Word were merely preparatory preliminaries.

5. *They will not be exclusive.* The invitation to come forward for personal ministry (of which there is no trace in apostolic ministry) radically alters the nature of a meeting – from corporate activity to individual experience, from mutual edification to personal satisfaction. The result is to divide the group into those who participate and those who don't. There is real pressure on the latter. At best, they feel left out; at worst, they feel guilty. Are they resisting the moving of God's Spirit? In many situations it requires considerable courage *not* to go forward. The greatest pressure of all is put on those who have genuine problems relating to what is happening at the front of the meeting, a conflict of conscience between loyalty to the fellowship and loyalty to their understanding of Scripture. An increasing number find this so painful they feel they cannot attend such meetings or even continue in membership. In extreme cases they are told they are in danger of committing the unforgivable sin (Matthew 12:24–32; i.e. calling the work of the Holy Spirit the work of the devil). Where is that Christian love which is considerate towards scruples of conscience in a fellow believer?

6. *They will not be misinterpreted.* This is the crux of the matter. Once they are perceived as human reactions they will be removed from the category of 'signs following'

(Mark 16:17–20). This will have two effects. Negatively, it will mean that they will not be used to gauge the effectiveness of any meeting or ministry. Some may be blessed without any such symptoms; others may experience the symptoms without being blessed. An honest assessment will admit that there is no inevitable correlation between what happens on the inside and the outside. Positively, this evaluation will leave the way open for the true signs, miracles and wonders, proofs of the power of God, to be manifested – healing sick bodies, casting out demons. It is these objective events which Scripture emphasises. Of course they are not so easy to produce for public inspection. Maybe that is why there has been such an eagerness to receive and reproduce the current symptoms – here was something we did seem able to do to demonstrate that God was with us. The desire to let people see as well as hear the Gospel is perfectly legitimate (Romans 15:18f.; 1 Corinthians 2:4; 1 Thessalonians 1:4–5). But we must be sure that we really are displaying the power of the kingdom in a way that is clearly of God and in line with apostolic teaching.

7. *They will not be homogenised.* I mean by this that they will not simply be accepted uncritically as all having the same significance. Since they are human reactions, we must ask, in each and every case, what was causing the reaction. Broadly speaking, there are always three possible sources of experience – the Lord, the flesh or the devil. It is also possible for these to get mixed together in varying proportions (just as, for example, a prophetic word can be a mixture of flesh and spirit, hence the need for it to be

carefully weighed and judged by others). This carefulness is especially necessary when we surrender control of ourselves into the *hands* of someone else. There is need for real discernment when 'channelling' is practised. This is not always easy because a 'mixture' may not be apparent at first. Is this why Timothy was told: 'Do not be hasty in the laying on of hands' (1 Timothy 5:22)? The other side of this coin might be: 'Do not be hasty to have hands laid on you.'

8. *They will not be sought.* The other guidelines in this chapter are mainly for leaders. This last one is for everybody. Seek God. Seek his blessing. But don't seek an experience for its own sake. Your reactions to a divine encounter may be quite different from other people's. I remember a dear older lady asking me to pray for her at the end of a meeting. When I asked her for her specific request, she replied: 'That I may fall down on the floor', adding wistfully: 'I've never fallen down yet.' I told her frankly I just couldn't ask the Lord to push her over, so I did not pray with her. I must be honest and complete the story. A few minutes later I found her lying on the floor with a beatific smile on her face! That humbled me more than her! But she is not the only one I have felt was seeking the assurance of a physical reaction. John Mumford, the Vineyard Fellowship leader in London, has openly stated that he has not observed a direct correlation between outward reactions and inward benefits of 'ministry'; some have been 'blessed' without 'manifestations', others have had 'manifestations' without being 'blessed'. The lesson is clear: seek God's blessing.

CHAPTER 10

A yellow light

A FAMILIAR educational principle states that if you can ask the right questions, you don't need the answers! I suppose it means that you are already thinking along the right lines and if you continue this course you will arrive at the right conclusions.

In this book I have tried to ask the right questions. Indeed, I believe its title is *the* right question, which warranted far more attention and discussion than it has received so far. Hopefully, my efforts may move it up on the agenda.

No doubt, some and perhaps many readers will be disappointed not to find a more clear-cut opinion, which can then be quoted (in approval or disapproval!). Others will understand why this has not been my objective.

So where does all this leave us? What signal am I sending out?

Most books on the subject already published have shone a *green* light, clearly indicating 'GO'. Enthusiastically advising us to go for it, to go all out for it, their counsel is very positive. This is probably the most significant 'move' of God's Spirit in our generation and no one can afford to miss out on it.

A few books have taken an opposite line and shone a *red* light, clearly indicating 'STOP'. Don't go any further. Don't get involved at all. Danger ahead. They see nothing but dangerous deception emanating from Toronto, capable of leading large sections of the Church into erroneous beliefs and behaviour.

I have switched on a *yellow* light, clearly indicating 'CAUTION'. The light could later change to red or green, but for the time being its message is: Proceed with caution!

After all, these are early days. At the time of writing, the 'Toronto' phenomenon has not yet reached its second birthday. The extraordinary speed with which it has spread (partly due to modern communications, particularly air travel!) has hardly given enough time to think. But we do need to be thinking as well as talking about it.

Surprisingly, both enthusiasm for and criticism of 'Toronto' can have a negative effect. That needs amplification.

On the one hand, uncritical enthusiasm can damage the work of the Spirit by bringing it into disrepute. One of the saddest effects, to me, has been on evangelicals who were at first highly suspicious of the charismatic renewal, but were persuaded by a sound appeal to Scripture to become part of it. A number of them have now said they don't want to be identified by the label 'charismatic' or associated with its current development. This has confirmed their worst fears – that experience would become the basis of theology and that 'prophecies' would become more highly regarded than Scripture. They are reverting to noncharismatic and even anti-charismatic stances. As one of those who for years pleaded for an openness to the charismatic dimension of the New Testament, I grieve over this development and cannot regard it as anything but a retrograde step.

On the other hand, I realise full well that negative criticism can also cause people to hold back. Jesus himself knew that fear of 'getting the wrong thing' can prevent someone from receiving the right gift from the heavenly Father (see his reassurance on this point in Luke 11:11–13).

I would be equally unhappy if the cumulative effect of this detailed examination of the 'Toronto blessing' was to leave anyone so uncertain or confused about what is or is not of the Spirit that they opted out of seeking any deeper experience of the Spirit.

Of one thing I am sure: we must not let either positive or negative reactions discourage us from hungering and thirsting for all that God has promised us in Scripture and conveys to us by the power of his Holy Spirit.

In an earlier chapter (4), I have outlined the biblical work of the Spirit, in which I firmly believe. Experiencing baptism in the Spirit and exercising gifts of the Spirit are the birthright of every penitent believer. Both his gifts and his fruit are essential to building up the Church of Christ. We must not be distracted from any of these, though I confess I have found it more difficult to preach about them in recent months because of the preoccupation with 'Toronto'. Some congregations seem unable to contemplate any other mode of the Spirit's operation for the time being.

However, novelty wears off. The early excitement of

new experiences is bound to decline. Frequent and lengthy 'blessing' meetings must sooner or later give way to a more balanced programme, hopefully without losing anything of lasting value that has been gained.

My fear is that in the meanwhile great damage could have been done to the unity of the body of Christ. The polarising tendency of current discussion ('Are you for or against the Toronto blessing?') could realign Christians with a common belief in Word and Spirit. It certainly would be a tragedy if division took place over something with debatable, if not questionable, basis in Scripture.

There is great need for patience as well as honesty with one another. We need to share both our testimonies and our doubts in the openness of mutual love. Neither the enthusiastic nor the critical should be written off as gullible or stubborn. Motives should not be suspect unless they are clearly shown to be unworthy. Neither the good features nor the bad features of a new thing should be exaggerated. Above all, we need to give each other time to reach our own convictions; to rush anyone into an attitude that does not spring from their own judgment savours of manipulation.

It is my hope and prayer that this volume will take some heat out of the debate and shed some light (if only yellow!) on it. I want readers to make up their own minds, not just accept or quote mine. Perhaps running through all I've written is a call to be more discriminating in what we accept. Discernment, after all, is a gift of the Spirit (1 Corinthians 12:10). Tolerance and gullibility are not listed among Christian virtues.

Above all, we need the 'mind of Christ'. I don't mean his opinion about the 'blessing', though he must have one! In Scripture his 'mind' is his attitude to himself which governed his attitude to others – in a word, that humility that looks to the interests of others rather than one's own. Perhaps the best thing you can do after reading this book is to meditate on the first thirteen verses in the second chapter of Paul's letter to the Philippians. The kind of 'trembling' there described is thoroughly biblical and absolutely essential!

APPENDIX

History repeats itself

T HIS book has been concerned with biblical rather than historical precedents for the 'blessing'.

However, it is impossible to ignore the latter aspect, not least because most of those who have attempted a biblical defence have invariably moved quite swiftly from the apostles and prophets to 'authorities' many centuries later and outside Scripture – namely Jonathan Edwards, George Whitefield and John Wesley. All lived in the eighteenth century and saw a 'revival' spanning the Atlantic. Many of the current 'manifestations' were seen among the hearers of these preachers.

The eagerness with which contemporary 'apologetics' (reasoned defence) seize on these parallels to supplement Scripture suggests that the biblical basis is not really suffi-cient to establish the case (this book probably explains why). The emphatic appeal to 'tradition' is, to say the least, unusual among evangelicals. To put it simply, if there was a clear rationale for the 'blessing' in the teaching of Peter, Paul, James, John or Jesus himself, would anyone be talk-ing so much, or at all, about Jonathan Edwards?

Furthermore, the danger of 'proof-texting' (in the sense

of quoting texts out of context) is just as real when appealing to history as when appealing to Scripture. For example, Edwards' views on 'manifestations' are eagerly sought, in sharp contrast to the deafening silence about his strong preaching on hell, though it was often the latter which produced the former. And his earlier impressions may be selected rather than his mature reflections. The fact that both John and Charles Wesley both experienced a bout of laughter which they believed was of God may be quoted without mentioning that John's considered opinion was that most outbreaks of laughter in his meetings were of demonic origin. History, like Scripture, can be made to prove anything, when handled with subjective selection.

Those who have what might be called a 'theology of revival' are prone to assume that whatever happened during past times of spiritual fervour is therefore validated for today. But even 'revivals' must be tested in the light of Scripture, not least because in times of religious excitement the critical faculties are dulled and the possibilities of human substitute and satanic counterfeit are increased.

When we look more closely at the eighteenth-century revival, there are some important differences between the physical phenomena then and now.

The first is that they happened *during* the preaching of the Word rather than afterwards. They came as a spontaneous response to the message and usually indicated a strong conviction of sin and guilt. They were more associated with the fear of a holy God than the feeling of a loving God. As such, they were accepted (even welcomed?) by the evangelists – as signs that their Gospel was reaching the hearts of their hearers. People fell down under the power of the *Word*, rather than the power of the Spirit – or perhaps we should say both, operating together. It was, therefore, largely unbelievers who showed these symptoms. Would that this was happening on the same scale today!

The second, and more important, observation is that none of these men *encouraged* these reactions to their preaching and never sought to 'minister' them through prayer and laying-on hands. They let the Holy Spirit do his work and let the people respond as they would, not trying to manipulate either themselves. They only prayed for individuals *after* they 'manifested' such symptoms, assuming them to be signs of need rather than blessing. Falling down was a signal to start praying, not, as so often today, the moment to stop interceding!

The third point to underline is that they did not accept all these phenomena as proof of an encounter with God; they were more discerning than that. Knowing how eager and subtle is Satan's interference with a genuine work of God, they kept a sharp look-out for his deceptive devices.

The fourth way in which we can learn from them is that they did not focus attention on this aspect of their mission (their critics were only too ready to do so). Neither in their preaching nor their practice did they even hint that an experience of this kind was a desirable, much less a necessary, channel or confirmation of divine blessing. Calling such happenings the 'Bristol' or the 'Boston' blessing would probably have been anathema to Whitefield and

Wesley, who certainly preached an 'experimental' (what we would call an 'experiential') theology, but always defined genuine experience in biblical terminology.

As it happens, I paid a visit to Boston in the middle of writing this book and had the opportunity to visit many of the New England places affected by the eighteenth-century 'revival' there.

Among other interesting visits, I came across 'Shaker' villages – or what remains of them. Some are now museums, since only a few sisters remain of the thousands who lived in these communities for over two centuries.

Started by an illiterate woman in Manchester, 'Mother Annie Lee', as a reaction to the 'quietest' worship of early Quakers, they soon became notorious for their exuberance, singing and dancing with symbolic gestures (cupped hands held upwards for receiving blessing, shaken downwards to renounce sin) – hence the nickname 'Shaking Quakers' or 'Shakers'.

Persecuted in England, they fled to the 'New World' where, after initial setbacks, they began to hold camp meetings and eventually established 'villages' where they could live 'separate from the world' and devote themselves to the twin callings of work and worship.

Their buildings are models of functional simplicity, kept spotlessly clean. Their functional furniture has a dignity that now commands high prices in the antique market. Their ingenuity gave a number of inventions to the world, from the circular saw to the common clothes peg, water-resistant fabric to condensed milk. Their industrious lives were legendary. They renounced private property; and poverty, debt and unemployment were unknown among them (many took advantage of their hospitality during hard winters!). They believed in equal rights for men and women (with elders and elderesses), but men worked outdoors and women indoors.

But it was their meetings in which I was most interested, having so many features of what is now labelled 'charismatic' worship. In addition to spontaneous leaping and dancing (later formalised into various shuffling steps), some fell to the floor in 'trances'. At one stage they had outbursts of what they called a 'laughing spirit'.

Their numbers increased with converts from the 'Great Awakening' in 1740, many of whom were dissatisfied with their own churches. They adopted many orphans and brought them up as 'Shakers', though they had the choice to leave or 'sign the covenant' at maturity.

The one thing they couldn't have was 'biological' growth, since they renounced marriage along with property and lived strictly segregated lives as 'brothers and sisters'. This, and later laws restricting adoption, account for their steady decline to near extinction.

Apart from this requirement to abstain from marriage, their lifestyle would probably have wide appeal to charismatic Christians and their worship would probably be associated with 'Toronto'! Yet there were dangerous seeds of disintegration in their doctrines, which are a warning to us today.

Their meetings, for example, were almost entirely composed of singing and dancing. There were no sermons.

This absence of systematic teaching was undoubtedly one cause of their being led astray. But the main factor was false prophecy, particularly in the form of unchecked visions.

Their own title for themselves was: 'The United Society of Believers in Christ's Second Appearing'. This sounds orthodox, if a little unbalanced in singling out only one part of the Gospel – until it is realised that this was a reference to Annie Lee's advent! In her the 'parousia' of Christ had happened.

This led them to the belief that the millennium had now begun and the kingdom of heaven was re-established on earth (so their communal buildings were full of light and free of dust, as befits heaven!). This was one reason why they neither married nor were given in marriage (the other was a vision which 'Mother' Lee had of Adam and Eve having intercourse when a voice said: 'This was the original sin'; she had also regarded the stillbirths from her own four pregnancies as divine punishment for enjoying sex with her blacksmith husband).

Her strangely modern teaching that God had a female as well as a male nature and could be addressed as Mother and Father was the 'theological' basis for the 'equal' leadership of women and men in the communities, though 'elderesses' only had authority over the women.

It was, however, their vulnerability to any and all 'visions' or 'gifts' received in their meetings that led to their undoing. One such picture was of a crowd of Indians at the door of their meeting house, seeking access to their community. In the absence of any real Indians arriving, they assumed that they were to invite Indian spirits to attend their gatherings! It may not be a coincidence that that was when the 'laughing spirit' broke out among them.

Gradually they were drawn into what we now call 'spiritism' or 'spiritualism'. Later, they would claim that the Fox sisters, the founding mediums of spiritualist churches, were the fulfilment of Annie Lee's predictions.

I have included this rather sad tale of a noble venture to make a few necessary points about the appeal to history.

First, history is a mixed bag! It is easy to select the bits that suit our case and ignore the whole picture. Then our interpretation of what we have selected can lead to prejudiced conclusions. In the case above, it would obviously be quite wrong to deduce that all helpless laughter in Christian meetings is the influence of Indian spirits!

Second, and far more important, my encounter with the 'Shaker' tradition made me realise afresh how vital it is to maintain the regular ministry of teaching the whole Word of God, especially in the context of less inhibited worship, which makes the entrance of alien elements that much easier. 'Charismatic' freedom makes it even more necessary to 'test all things'.

Third, how dangerous it can be to put any other 'revelation' on a par with Scripture. This has been the fundamental error of the cults, from Mary Baker Eddy's 'Science and Health' (the huge headquarters are also in Boston) to Joseph Smith's golden tablets. To place Annie Lee's maxims, good though some of them were ('Hands to work and hearts to God' and 'Do all your work as though you had a thousand years to live and as you would if you knew you must die tomorrow'), on the same level as the teaching of Jesus was a fundamental error that was bound to result in heresy.

In a subtle way, we can fall into the same error by appealing to church history and to Scripture simultaneously, as if they carry similar authority. However inspiring the experience of the saints through the ages may be, it is not to be regarded in the same light as the inspired Word of God.

That is why these 'historical' comments are in an appendix, rather than a chapter in the main part of the book. It was another way of saying that historical appeals should be kept quite separate from biblical considerations.

We are all prone to see the past through rose-coloured spectacles, to talk of the 'good old days' (though few would choose to go back and live in them, if that were possible!). The Christian version of such nostalgia is to idealise, even idolise, a particular period in the pilgrimage of the Church that especially appeals to us. So we look back longingly at the Reformers or the Anabaptists or the Puritans or the Primitive Methodists or the early Pentecostals – consciously or unconsciously endeavouring to recover and relive the past. It is a futile quest. The clock cannot be turned back. History never actually repeats itself.

Our authority lies in the unchanging words which will never pass away, though heaven and earth vanish. Our task is to apply them to our own day and circumstances until all God's promises for the future are fulfilled.

Also by David Pawson

FOURTH WAVE

Charismatics and Evangelicals:
are we ready to come together?

Foreword by Clive Calver

For the last quarter of a century, Charismatics and Evangelicals have been moving closer together. The time is ripe, maintains David Pawson, for the two fastest-growing streams in Christendom to be fully integrated.

With personal experience of both and a passionate desire to see them united, David Pawson makes a searching study of their remaining differences which he believes can be resolved without compromise.

After defining and clarifying their respective positions, he addresses such critical points of divergence as theology and experience, prophecy and Scripture, initiation, tongues, ministry and holiness. The challenge for both, he maintains, is to reconsider their traditional understanding in the light of all the biblical data.

160 pages
ISBN 0 340 58042 9

Also by David Pawson

WHEN JESUS RETURNS

*What is known about Christ's second coming
and how can we prepare for it?*

Christians everywhere await Christ's return. Will he come
to the whole world or just one place? Soon and suddenly
or after clear signs? What can he achieve by coming back
here and how long will it take?

David Pawson brings clarity and insight to these and
many other vital issues surrounding the bodily return of
Jesus Christ to our world, a subject which will continue to
dominate the Church's agenda as the end of the millennium approaches. Based on a new approach to the interpretation of the book of Revelation, the controversial subjects
of the 'Rapture' and the 'Millennium' are discussed in de-
tail, completing this vital resource for our times.

274 pages
ISBN 0 340 61211 8